The Art
of Fencing, or, The
Use of the Small Sword

Monsieur L'Abbat

Translated by Andrew Mahon

The ART of

FENCING,

or, the USE of the

Small SWORD.

Translated from the FRENCH of the late celebrated

Monsieur L'ABBAT;

Master of that ART at the Academy of TOULOUSE.

By ANDREW MAHON, Professor of the SMALL SWORD in
DUBLIN.

Contents

DEDICATION.

PREFACE.

CHAP. I. *Of chusing and mounting a* Blade.

CHAP. II. *Of Guard.*

CHAP. III. *Of Pushing Quart.*

CHAP. IV. *Of the Parade of Quart.*

CHAP. V. *Of pushing* Tierce *without, or on the Outside of the Sword.*

CHAP. VI. *Of pushing* Seconde.

CHAP. VII. *The Parades of* Seconde.

CHAP. VIII. *Of* Quart *under the Wrist.*

CHAP. IX. *Of* Flanconnade.

CHAP. X. *Of* Parades.

CHAP. XI. *Of the* demarches, *or manner of advancing and retiring.*

CHAP. XII. *Of* Disengagements.

CHAP. XIII. *Of* Feints.

CHAP. XIV. *Of cutting over the Point of the* Sword.

CHAP. XV. *Of the* Reprise, *or redoubled Thrust.*

CHAP. XVI. *Of passing* Quarte *within the Sword.*

CHAP. XVII. *Of passing* Quarte *within the Sword.*

CHAP. XVIII. *Of Joining or seizing the* Sword.

CHAP. XIX. *Of engaging in* Quarte *in a midling Guard.*

CHAP. XX. *Of engaging in* Tierce *in the Midling Guard.*

CHAP. XXI. Of several Guards, and the Manner of attacking them.

CHAP. XXII. *Of Left-handed Men.*

CHAP. XXIII. *Of the Parade of the Hand.*

CHAP. XXIV. *Of the beat of the Foot, in closing the measure, or in the same place.*

CHAP. XXV. *Of the Good Effects of a nice Discernment of the Eye.*

CHAP. XXVI. *Of Time.*

CHAP. XXVII. *Of Swiftness.*

CHAP. XXVIII. *Of Measure.*

CHAP. XXIX. *Of the Necessity of some Qualities in a Master.*

CHAP. XXX. *Rules for pushing and parrying at the Wall, and for making an Assault.*

CHAP. XXXI. *Against several erroneous Opinions.*

Thrusts of Emulation for Prizes, Wagers &c.

FOOTNOTES

DEDICATION.

[Section missing]

        sue for. I shall omit saying any Thing, My Lord, of the shining Qualities, which seem Hereditary in Your Lordship's Family, as well as of the Dignity and Importance of the Charge with which His Majesty has been pleased to entrust Your Lordship's Most Noble Father. Neither will I presume to trouble Your Lordship with those Encomiums, which are most deservedly due to the Vertues, whereby Your Lordship has gained the Admiration and Esteem of the Polite and Ingenious Persons of this Nation. Be pleased then, My Lord, to permit me to have the Honour of subscribing myself,

My Lord,

Your Lordship's

Most devoted, and

Most humble

Servant,

Andrew Mahon.

PREFACE.

I thought it very suitable to my Business, when I met with so good an Author as Monsieur *L'Abbat*, on the Art of Fencing, to publish his Rules, which in general, will I believe be very useful, not only as they may contribute to the Satisfaction of such Gentlemen as are already Proficients in the Art, and to the better Discipline of those who intend to become so, but also in regard that the Nicety and Exactness of his Rules, for the most Part, and their great Consistency with Reason, may, and will in all Probability, lay a regular and good Foundation for future Masters, who tho' accustom'd to any particular Method formerly practised, may rather chuse to proceed upon the Authority of an excellent Master, than upon a vain and mistaken Confidence of their own Perfection, or upon an obstinate Refusal to submit to Rules founded on, and demonstrated by Reason.

For my Part, though I had my Instructions from the late Mr. *Hillary Tully* of *London*, who was (and I think with great Reason) esteemed a most eminent Master in his Time, I thought I could not make too nice a Scrutiny into my Profession, by comparing Notes with Monsieur *L'Abbat*, which improved me in some Points, and confirmed me and others, to my no small Satisfaction, being well persuaded, that, as a Professor of this Science, it would have been an unpardonable Fault in me to deprive our Nations of such an Improvement, either through Prejudice to his, or Partiality to my own Opinion.

Though I have already said that Mr. *L'Abbat's* Rules are nice, reasonable, and demonstrative, yet I would not have it inferred from thence, that he approves of them all, as really essential to the Art of Fencing; there being some which he does not approve of, and which he would not have mentioned, had they not interfered with his profession, by the Practice and Recommendation of some Masters, who being more capricious than knowing, were fonder of the shewy or superficial, than of the solid Part of the Science.

Volting, Passing, and Lowering the Body, are three things which Mr. *L'Abbat* disapproves of, in which Opinion I join; because the Sword being the Instrument of Defence, there can be no Safety when the proper Opposition of the Blade is wanting, as it is in volting and lowering the Body, and in passing, by reason of the Weakness of the Situation, which cannot produce a vigorous Action.

Notwithstanding which, there is a modern Master, who as soon as he had seen this Book, and the Attitudes representing volting, passing and lowering the Body, began and still continues teaching them to his Scholars, without considering how unsafe and dangerous they are, for want of the proper Opposition of the Sword when within Measure.

Of all Professions, that of Arms has in all Ages, since their Invention, been esteemed the noblest and most necessary; it being by them that the Laws preserve their Force, that our Dominions are defended from the Encroachments of our Enemies, and ill designing People kept in the Subjection due to their Sovereigns; and of all Arms, the Sword is probably the most ancient: It is honourable and useful, and upon Occasion, causes a greater Acquisition of Glory than any other: It is likewise worn by Kings and Princes, as an Ornament to Majesty and Grandeur, and a Mark of their Courage, and distinguishes the Nobility from the lower Rank of Men.

It is the most useful, having the Advantage of Fire Arms, in that it is as well defensive as offensive, whereas they carry no Defence with them; and it is far preferable to Pikes and other long Weapons, not only because it is more weildy and easy of Carriage, but also by reason of the Perfection to which Art has brought the Use of the Small Sword; there being no Exercise that conduces so much as Fencing, to strengthen and supple the Parts, and to give the Body an easy and graceful Appearance.

The Sword, since it's first Invention, has been used in different Manners: First, with a Shield or Buckler; Secondly, with a Helmet, and Thirdly, with a Dagger, which is still used in *Spain* and *Italy*. Mr. *Patinotris*, who taught at *Rome*, introduced, and laid down Rules for the Use of the Small Sword alone, which has since been much improved by the *French* and our Nations.

As the Art of Fencing consists in attacking and defending with the Sword, it is necessary that every Motion and Situation tend to these two principal Points, *viz.* In offending to be defended, and in defending to be in an immediate Condition to offend.

There is no Guard but has it's Thrust, and no Thrust without it's Parade, no Parade without it's Feint, no Feint without it's opposite Time or Motion, no opposite Time or Motion but has it's Counter, and there is even a Counter to that Counter.

Some injudicious Persons have objected to Mr. *L'abbat's* Manner of Fencing, that it is too beautiful and nice, without observing that if it be beautiful, it cannot be dangerous, Beauty consisting in Rule, and Rule in the Safety of attacking and defending.

In Fencing, there are five Figures of the Wrist, *viz. Prime, Seconde, Tierce, Quart,* and *Quinte.* The first is of very little Use, and the last of none at all.

Prime is the Figure that the Wrist is in, in drawing the Sword. *Seconde* and *Tierce* require one and the same Figure of the Wrist, with this Difference only, that in *Seconde,* the Wrist must be raised higher, in order to oppose the Adversary's Sword; but in both these Thrusts the Thumb Nail must be turned directly down, and the Edges of the Blade of the Foil of an equal Height.

Quart is the handsomest Figure in Fencing, the Thumb Nail and the Flat of the Foil being directly up, and the Wrist supported so as to cover the Body below as well as above. In *Quinte,* the Wrist is more turned and raised that in *Quart,* which uncovers the Body, and weakens the Point, and therefore is not used by the skilful.

Some Masters divide the Blade into three Parts, *viz.* the Fort, the Feeble, and the Middle. Others divide it into Four, *viz.* the Fort, the Half Fort, the Feeble, and the Half Feeble; but to avoid Perplexity, I divide it only into Fort and Feeble; tho' it may be divided into as many Parts as there are Degrees of Fort and Feeble to be found on the Blade.

The Attitudes which are in the Book, are copied exactly from the Originals; tho' I might perhaps have made some Alterations, in my

Opinion, for the better, yet I chose rather to leave them as they are, than to run the Hazard of spoiling any of them: I have therefore left the same Bend in the Foils as Mr. *L'Abbat* recommends, *and for which he makes an Apology in his Preface.*

Nor have I, in any of the Attitudes, represented a Left-handed Figure, because by looking thro' the Paper on the blank Side, they will appear reversed, and consequently Left-handed.

Monsieur *L'Abbat* recommends the turning on the Edge of the Left-foot in a Lunge, as may be seen by the Attitudes. This Method indeed was formerly practised by all Masters, and would be very good, if their Scholars had not naturally run into an Error, by turning the Foot so much as to bring the Ancle to the Ground, whereby the Foot became so weak as to make the Recovery difficult, for want of a sufficient Support from the Left-foot, which, in recovering, bears the whole Weight of the Body: Therefore I would not advise the turning on the Edge of the Foot to any but such as, by long Practice on the Flat, are able to judge of the Strength of their Situation, and consequently, will not turn the Foot more than is consistent therewith.

It may sometimes be necessary to turn on the Edge, on such Ground whereon the Flat would slip, and the Edge would not, if it were properly turned; but even in this Case, by turning it too much it would have no Hold of the Terrace, and therefore would be as dangerous as keeping it on the Flat.

The chief Reason for turning on the Edge, is that the Length of the Lunge is greater by about three Inches, which a Man who is a Judge of Measure need never have recourse to, because he will not push but when he knows he is within Reach.

Some of the Subscribing Gentlemen will, perhaps, be surprized, when they find this Book published in my Name, after having taken Receipts, for the first Moiety of their Subscription Money, in the Name of Mr. *Campbell*, to whom I am obliged for his Assistance in the Translation, he being a better Master of the *French* Tongue than I am. Indeed to the chief Reasons why they were not signed in my Name, are, First, because I was, at the Time of their being signed, a

Stranger in this city, being then lately come from *England*. And secondly, lest I should meet with such Opposition as might perhaps have frustrated my Design of publishing this book, I thought proper to conceal my being concerned in it, 'till Mr. *Campbell* had shown the Translation to all the principal Masters in Town, and gained their Approbation much in Favour of it.

CHAP. I.

Of chusing and mounting a Blade.

Courage and Skill being often of little Use without a good Weapon, I think it necessary, before I lay down Rules for using it, to shew how to chuse a good Blade, and how it ought to be mounted.

The Length of the Blade ought to be proportionable to the Stature of the Person who is to use it: The longest Sword, from Point to Pommel, should reach perpendicularly from the Ground to the Navel, and the shortest, to the Waste; being large in Proportion to its Length, and not extremely large, nor very small, as some People wear them; the over large Blades being unweildy, unless very hollow, which makes them weak, and the narrow ones being not sufficient to cover the Body enough.

In Order to chuse a good Blade, three Things are to be observed: First, that the Blade have no Flaw in it, especially across, it being more dangerous so than Length-way. Secondly, That it be well tempered, which you'll know by bending it against a Wall or other Place; if it bend only towards the Point, 'tis faulty, but if it bend in a semicircular Manner, and the Blade spring back to its Straitness, 'tis a good Sign; If it remains bent it is a Fault, tho' not so great as if it did not bend at all; for a Blade that bends being of a soft Temper, seldom breaks; but a stiff One being hard tempered is easily broke. The third Observation is to be made by breaking the Point, and if the

Part broken be of a grey Colour, the Steel is good; if it be white 'tis not: Or you may strike the Blade with a Key or other Piece of Iron, and if he gives a clear Sound, there is no hidden Fault in it. In bending a Blade you must not force it, what I have said being sufficient to know it by, and besides by forcing it, it may be so weakened in some Part as to break when it comes to be used.

It would not be amiss for a Man to see his Sword mounted, because the Cutlers, to save themselves the Trouble of filing the inside of the hilts and pommel, to make the Holes wider, often file the Tongue[1] of the Blade too much, and fill up the Vacancies with Bits of Wood, by which Means the Sword is not firm in the Hand, and the tongue being thin and weak, is apt to break in Parrying or on a dry Beat, as has been unhappily experienced. Care should also be taken that the End of the Tongue be well riveted to the Extremity of the Pommel, lest the Grip should fly off, which would be of very dangerous Consequence.

Some Men chuse strait Blades, others will have them bending a little upwards or downwards; some like them to bend a little in the Fort, and others in the Feeble, which is commonly called *le Tour de Breteur*, or the Bullie's Blade. The Shell should be proportionable in Bigness to the Blade, and of a Metal that will resist a Point, and the Handle fitted to the Hand.

Some like square Handles, and others chuse round Ones; the square are better and firmer in the Hand, but as this Difference depends on Fancy, as does also the Bow, which in some Cases may preserve the Hand, but may be a Hindrance in inclosing, I shall leave it to the Decision of the Fashions.

CHAP. II.

Of Guard.

By Guard, is meant such a Situation of all the Parts of the Body as enables them to give their mutual Assistance to defend or attack. A Guard cannot be perfect without a good and graceful Disposition, proceeding from a natural Proportion of the Parts of the Body, and an easy and vigorous Motion, which is to be acquired by Practice, and the Instruction of a good Master.

As In all bodily Excercises, a good Air, Freedom, Vigour, and a just Disposition of the Body and Limbs are necessary, so are they more especially in Fencing, the least Disorder in this Case being of the worst Consequence; and the Guard being the Center whence all the Vigour should proceed, and which should communicate Strength and Agility to every Part of the Body, if there be the least Irregularity in any one Part, there cannot be that Agreeableness, Power of Defence, Justness, or Swiftness that is requisite.

In order to be well in Guard, it is absolutely necessary that the Feet, as the Foundation that conduces chiefly to communicate Freedom and Strength to the other Parts, be placed at such a Distance from each other, and in such a lineal Manner as may be advantageous: The Distance must be about two Foot from one Heel to the other; for if it were greater, the Adversary, tho' of the same Stature, and with a Sword of equal Length, would be within Measure when you would not, which would be a very considerable Fault, Measure being one of the principal Parts of Fencing, and if the Feet were nearer together, you would want Strength, which is also a great Fault, because a feeble Situation cannot produce a vigorous Action.

The Line must be taken from the hindmost Part of the Right Heel to the Left Heel near the Ancle. The Point of the Right Foot must be opposite to the Adversary's, turning out the Point of the Left Foot, and bending the Left Knee over the Point of the same Foot, keeping the Right Knee a little bent, that it may have a Freedom of Motion.

1st. Plate

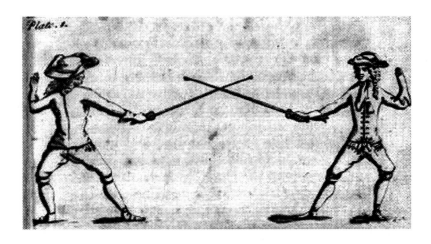

The middling Guard.

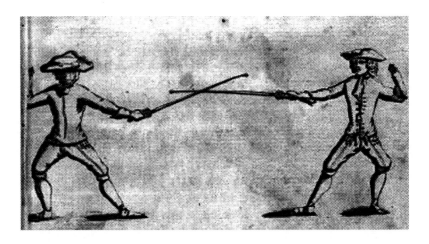

The straight Guard or flat Sword.

The Body must be upright, which gives it a better Air, greater Strength, and more Liberty to advance and retire, being supported almost equally by the two Feet. Some Masters teach to keep the Body back in Favour of Measure, which cannot be broke by the Body when 'tis already drawn back, tho' it is often necessary, not only to avoid a Surprize, but also to deceive a Man of superior Swiftness who pushes a just Length: Therefore 'tis much better to have the Liberty of retiring to avoid the Thrusts of the Adversary, or of extricating yourself by advancing towards him and pushing (as I shall observe in its proper Place) than to keep the Body in one Situation at a Distance, which being fixed, cannot deceive a Person who knows any thing of Measure; moreover, such a Retention of the Body does not only hinder the breaking Measure with the Body, but also the Left Leg is so oppressed with its whole Weight, that it would find it difficult to retire upon Occasion.

The Elbows must be almost on a Line, and of an equal Height, that one Shoulder may not be higher than the other, and that they may be both turn'd alike; the Left Hand must be over against the Top of the Ear, the Hilt of the Sword a little above the Hip, turning towards Half *Quart*, the Thumb extended, pressing the Middle of the Eye of the Hilt, keeping the Fingers pretty close to the Handle, especially the little one, in order to feel the Sword firmer and freer in the Hand.

By feeling the Sword, is meant commanding the Fort and Feeble equally with the Hand, in order to communicate to the more distant Part of the Blade, as well as to that which is nearer, the Motion and Action that is requisite.

The Hilt should be situated in the Center, that is to say, between the upper and lower Parts, and the Inside and Outside of the Body, in order to be in a better Condition to defend whatever Part may be attacked. The Arm must not be strait nor too much bent, to preserve its Liberty and be cover'd. The Parts being thus placed, the Wrist and the Point of the Right Foot will be on a perpendicular Line.

The Point of the Sword ought to be about the Height of, and on a Line with the Adversary's Shoulder, that is, it must be more or less raised, according as he is taller or shorter: Some Masters raise it to one fixed Height, which would be very well if all Men were of the same Stature; but if we consider the difference in Height of Persons, we shall find it evidently bad. 'Tis to be observed, that according to the Length or Shortness of the Blade, the Line from the Shell to the Point is higher or lower, when the Height of the Point is fix'd.

The Shoulder, the Bend of the Arm, the Hilt, the Point of the Sword, the Hip, the Right Knee and the Point of the Right Foot must be on a Line.

The Head should be upright and free without Stiffness or Affectation, the Face turned between full and profile, and not altogether full, as many Masters will have it, that being a constrained and disagreeable Figure.

The Sight should be fixed on the Adversary's, not only to observe his Motions, but also to discover his Design, it being possible to guess at the interior Design, by the exterior Action.

It is necessary to appear animated with a brave Boldness, for nothing requires a Man to exert himself more than Sword in Hand; and it is as difficult to attain such an Air of Intrepidity without much Excercise, as it is to become perfectly expert.

2d Plate.

A Lunge in Quart.

A Thrust in Quart.

CHAP. III.

Of Pushing Quart.

To push *Quart* within, besides the Precautions of placing yourself to Advantage, and of pushing properly and swiftly, which is to be acquired by Practice and nice Speculation, It is necessary that the Parts, in order to assist each other in making the Thrust, should be so disposed and situated, as that the Wrist should draw with it the Bend of the Arm, the Shoulder, and the upper Part of the Fore-Part of the Body, at the same time that the Left Hand and Arm should display or stretch themselves out smartly, bending one of the Knees and extending the other, which gives more Vigour and Swiftness to the Thrust; and the Body finding itself drawn forward by the swift Motion of the Wrist and other Parts, obliges the Right Foot to go forward in order to support it, and to give the Thrust a greater Length; the Left Foot should, at the same Instant, turn on the Edge, without stirring from its Place; whilst the Right Foot coming smartly to the Ground, finishes the Figure, Extension and Action of the Lunge. This is the Order and Disposition of the Parts in making the Thrust, which see in the second Plate. At the Instant when the Wrist moves forward, it must do three things, turn, support and oppose.

To turn the Wrist in *Quart*, the Thumb Nail must be up, and the inside Edge equal in Height with the other, for if it were not so high, the Thrust would not be so swift, for want of Motion enough, neither would the Body be so well covered, because the Edge, instead of being directly opposite to the Adversary's Sword, would fall off with a Slant; and if it were higher, it would make a Quint Figure, which, by the excessive Turn of the Wrist, would weaken the Thrust, and by the unequal Turn of the Edges would uncover the Body.

The Wrist ought to be of a Height sufficient to cover the Body without contracting the Arm, which cannot be fixed to a particular Height; for a short Man against a tall one, should raise it as high as the Head, which People of equal; Stature, or a tall Man against a short one, ought not to do.

When the Opposition is accompanied with such a Turn and Support of the Wrist as will cover the Body, it is good, but if the Wrist be carried too far in, you not only lose Part of the Length of the Thrust, but also uncover the Outside of the Body, which are two very great Faults.

The Thrust must be made on the Inside of the Right Shoulder, in order to take the Feeble with your Fort, and that you may be covered, bearing on the Adversary's Sword, by which Means, the Thrust will be well planted, and you less liable to receive one, which Advantages you lose by pushing otherwise.

In order to make the Thrust perfect, it must have its proper Strength and Support when planted: The Strength, is the Vigour with which the Thrust is made, and the Support is the Consequence of the Motion of the Wrist, turning and bearing upwards, which makes the Foil to bend accordingly, fixing itself 'till you retire.

The Foil may bend upwards in two Manners; the best Way for it to bend, is from the Middle towards the Button; the other Way is, when almost all the Blade makes a Semi-circle. The first has a better Effect, the Feeble being stronger, the other makes a greater Show; but the Point being feeble, there is not the same Advantage in the Thrust.

In all Thrusts, the Button should hit before the Right Foot comes to the Ground, and the Left Hand and Arm be stretched out smartly, to help the Body forward, and give more Swiftness to the Thrust: The Left Hand should always be conformable to the Right, turning to *Quart* or *Tierce*, according to the Thrust. The Left Hand and Arm should be on a Line with the Thigh, and their Height a little lower than the Shoulder.

The Body must lean a little forward before, to give the Thrust a greater Length; the Hips must not be so much bent as other Times; which weakens and shortens the Thrust, by the Distance which the lowering the Body causes from the Height of the Line which must come from the Shoulder; besides 'tis harder to recover, and you, by that Means, give the Adversary an Opportunity of taking your Feeble with his Fort, your Situation being very low. The Front of the Body should be hid by turning the two Shoulders equally on a Line.

The Foot should go out strait; in order to preserve the Strength and Swiftness of the Thrust, it must have its proper Line and Distance. The Line must be taken from the Inside of the Left Heel to the Point of the Adversary's Right Foot; If it turn inward or outward, the Button will not go so far, the strait Line being the shortest; besides the Body would be uncovered, for by carrying the Foot inwards, the Flank is exposed, and by carrying it outwards the Front of the Body, and the Body is thereby weakened; the Prop and the Body being obliged to form an Angle instead of a strait Line, from the Heel of the Left Foot to the Point or Button of the Foil.

In order to know the Distance of the Lunge, the Right Knee being bent, must form a perpendicular Line with the Point of the Foot; if the Foot were not so forward, the Heel would be off the Ground, and the Body would have less Strength, and if it were carried farther the Body could not easily bend it self, and consequently could not extend so far; moreover, it would want Strength, being at too great a Distance from the perpendicular Line of the Foot and Leg, which are its Support, and its Recovery would be more difficult.

The Foot should fall firm without lifting it too high, that the Soal of the Sandal, or Pump, may give a smart Sound, which not only looks better and animates more, but also makes the Foot firm, and in a Condition to answer the Swiftness of the Wrist.

Care must be taken not to carry the Point of the Foot inward or outward, because the Knee bending accordingly, as part of the Thigh, goes out of the Line of the Sword, and consequently, of the Line of Defence, besides 'tis very disagreeable to the Sight.

The Feet sometimes slip in the Lunge, the Right Foot sliding forward, or the Left backward; the first is occasioned by carrying out the Foot before the Knee is bent, whereas when the Knee brings it forward, it must fall flat and firm; the other proceeds from the Want of a sufficient Support on the Left Foot.

The Head should follow the Figure of the Body; when this is upright, that should be so to; when the Body leans, the Head must lean; when you push within, you must look at your Adversary on the Outside of your Arm, which is done without turning the Head, by the Opposition of the Hand only.

That every Thrust may carry with it it's due Extent and Strength, the Opposition of the Sword, the true placing of the Body, and a Facility of recovering; you are to observe that the two first are for Offence, and the others for Defence.

Every Thrust must have it's just Length, and carry with it a good Air, a regular Situation, Vigour, and a due Extension; *See the 2d. plate.*

Of recovering in Guard.

As soon as the Thrust is made, you must recover in *Guard*, which is done either by retiring out of Measure, or only to the Place from whence you, pushed; if out of Measure, 'tis done by springing back, or by bringing the Right Foot back behind the Left, and the Left behind the Right; and if to the Place from whence you pushed, you must parry if there's a Thrust made; and if not, you must command the Feeble of the Adversary's Sword, in order to cover the Side on which it is, without giving an Open on the other Side, which is done as you recover, by drawing back the Body on the Left Foot; which should bring with it the Right Knee, drawing the Foot, with the Heel a little raised from the Ground, to prevent any Accident that may happen by the Badness of the Terrace.

By this Recovery, commanding the Adversary's Sword, you either get Light if he not stir, or Time if he does, which instead of being dangerous, as has formerly been thought, it is, by the Help of Art, become advantageous.

CHAP. IV.

Of the Parade of Quart.

To parry, signifies, in our Art, to cover when the Adversary pushes, that Part which he endeavors to offend; which is done it either by the Opposition of the Sword or of the Left Hand; but as I am now speaking of the Sword only, I must observe; that in order to parry well with it, you are to take notice of the Manner and Swiftness of your Adversary: By the Manner, is meant whether in *Quart* or *Tierce*; with his Fort to your Feeble, or with his Feeble to your Fort; and you are to observe the Swiftness of his Thrust, that you may regulate your Parade accordingly.

When a Thrust is made with the Fort to your Feeble, which is the best way; you must, by raising and turning the Hand a little in *Quart*, raise the Point, which brings it nearer to you, and hinders the Adversary from gaining your Feeble, which being raised up is too far from him, and makes it easy for you to seize his Feeble. (Refer to the 3d. Plate.)

If the Thrust be made on the Fort or Middle of your Sword, you need only turn the Hand a little in *Quart*.

If after the Adversary has pushed *Quart*, he pushes *Seconde*; you must parry with the Fort, bringing it nearer to you, and for the greater Safety, or to avoid other Thrusts, or the taking Time on your return, you must oppose with the left Hand, which hinders him from hitting you as he meets your Thrust, and from parrying it, for want of having his Sword at Liberty. (Refer to the 7th Plate.)

The same Opposition may be made on a Lunge in *Quart*, and to be more safe in returning Thrust or Thrusts, you must close the Measure in parrying, which confounds the Enemy, who finds himself too near to have the Use of his Sword: Your Sword, in parrying, must carry it's Point lower and more inward than in the other Parades.

3rd Plate.

Parade of Quart.

Parade of Quart opposing with the Hand.

4th. Plate.

A Lunge in Tierce

Tierce Parryed.

If the Adversary makes a Thrust, with shortning or drawing back his Arm, or leaving his Body open; you must defend with the Left Hand, and lunge strait on him, unless you had rather parry with the Sword, making use of the Opposition of the Hand, and closing the Measure, as I just now observed.

You may also parry in disengaging,[2] drawing back the Body to the Left, in order to give the Hand Time and Facility to make the Parade.

There are several other Parades, of which I shall treat in their proper Places, confining myself now to the most essential.

CHAP. V.

Of pushing Tierce *without, or on the Outside of the Sword.*

In order to push *Tierce* well, the Hand being gone first, taking the Feeble with the Fort, turning down the Nails, and the Wrist a little outwards, not too high or low; in order not to give Light above or below, the Body must bend more forward and inward than in *Quart*; the Left Hand should extend itself in *Tierce*, because it ought, in all Cases, to be conformable with the Right, except that it is lower. When you push *Tierce*, you should look within your Sword: As to the Feet, they must be, in every Lunge, on the same Line, and at the same Distance.

The Rules I have laid down for recovering in *Quart*, will serve also in *Tierce*, but of the contrary Side.

Parade of Tierce.

To parry a Thrust made with the Fort to the Feeble, you must turn the whole Hand, carrying it a little outwards, raising the Point, in order to avoid the Adversary's taking your Feeble, and at the same time take His. *See the 4th* Plate.

If a Thrust be made on the Middle, or Fort of your Sword, you need only turn the Hand, carrying all the Blade equally outwards. Some Masters teach to parry this Thrust with the Hand in *Quart*, which is very dangerous if the Enemy pushes *Quart* over the Arm in the Fort, or *Quart* within, in the Feeble, there being an Opening in one, as well as the other Case; besides the Point is too far from the Line, to make a quick Return.

To avoid the Return of a Thrust when you have pushed *Tierce*, and that the Adversary, in parrying, has gained to your Feeble; you must, by raising and opposing with the Fort, bring the Pommel of your Sword on high; so that the Point be downwards; whereby his Point will be near your Left Shoulder, and you, not only avoid being hit,

5th. Plate.

Parade of Tierce yeilding the Feeble.

The same parade & opposition of the Hand.

but you may make a Thrust at the same time, by opposing with the Left Hand, and for the greater Safety, you must return on the Blade, and push strait, without quitting it. *See the 5th* Plate.

When a Thrust is made in *Tierce* upon the Blade on the Feeble, or by disengaging; tho' the first is more easily parryed, you must yeild the Feeble, opposing with the Fort, in order to guide the Adversary's Sword to the Place the most convenient for the Opposition of the Left Hand, and closing the Measure at the same time, you have an Opportunity, before he can recover, to hit him several times; which must be done by advancing on him, as fast as he retires. *See the 5th* Plate.

You may also parry by disengaging, drawing the Body back. The Return is easy, by pushing *Quart*; and to avoid a second Thrust from the Enemy at the Time of your Return, you must oppose with the Left Hand. *See the 5th* Plate.

CHAP. VI.

Of pushing Seconde.

In pushing under, the Hand must be turned in *Seconde*, as high as in *Quart*, and more within than in *Tierce*; the Body should be more bent, lower, and more forward than in thrusting *Tierce*, and the Left Hand lower. *See the 6th* Plate.

Seconde ought not be pushed, but on the following Occasions: First, when an Engagement, *Feint* or *Half-Thrust*, is made without, that the Adversary at one of these Times parrys high. Secondly, when your Adversary engages your Sword on the Outside, with his Hand raised high; or on the Inside, with his Feeble only; and thirdly, upon a Thrust or Pass, within or without.

The Recovery in Guard, should be in *Quart* within the Arm, though most Masters teach to recover on the Outside, which takes much more Time, and though the *Seconde* is independent on the Side, it is nearer to the Inside than to the Outside; because the Adversary carries his Wrist to the Outside, when he gives an Opportunity of making this Thrust; therefore you ought to return to his Sword in the shortest Time, in order to be sooner on your Guard. If you examine this Parade, you will find it is the only Means of recovering with Safety.

What introduced the Manner of returning to the Sword on the Outside, was the false Method formerly used in parrying the *Seconde* by beating on the Blade; in *Tierce*, with the Point downwards; so that the Adversary not being able to return but above, there was a Necessity for returning to the Sword on the Outside in order to defend; but the Parade and Return being no longer the same, the Manner of returning to the Sword must also be different.

CHAP. VII.

The Parades of Seconde.

Seconde may be parried three Ways. First, according to the ancient Manner I just described, which is done by a Semi-circle on the Inside, with the Hand in *Tierce*, the Point low, almost on a Line with the Wrist; but the Greatness of the Motion does not only render it difficult to parry the Thrust but still harder to parry the Feint of the Thrust and come up again; besides the *Rispost* is dangerous; because it requires a long Time to raise the Point, which is almost as low as the Ground, to the Body; in which Time, the Adversary has not only an Opportunity of parrying the Thrust, but also of hitting you whilst you are bringing up your Point.

Secondly, *Seconde* may be parryed by making a Half-circle on the Outside, the Wrist in *Quart*, as high as the Shoulder, the Arm extended, and the Point very low. *See the 7th* Plate. It is less dangerous, and more easy for the *Rispost* than the former, which must be made as soon as you have parryed, by pushing strait in *Quart* which the Adversary having pushed under, can hardly avoid, but by yeilding, and battering the Sword. *See the 7th* Plate.

To this Manner of parrying *Seconde*, there is but one Opposite, which is done by *feinting* below, and as the Adversary is going to cross your Sword, in order to parry, you must disengage by a little Circle, with the Hand in *Seconde*, which preventing the Enemy's Sword, gives an Opportunity of hitting him above, if the Wrist is lower than I have observed, or in *Flanconnade*, if the Wrist is high. A Man that parrys below, in order to avoid this *Feint*, must redouble his Circle to meet the Blade. This Parade is best in recovering, after having pushed, not only to avoid the strait or low *Rispost*, but also any Feint or Thrust.

The third and best Parade, is made with your Fort to the Middle of the Adversary's Sword, the Wrist turned in *Quart*, but a little lower: The *Rispost* of this Parade is very good, when you know how to bind the Sword upon the *Rispost*; and it cannot be parryed without returning to the Parade that I have here, before, described and which, I believe, is peculiar to myself.

This Parade is by so much the more adventageous, as the *Rispost* is easy the Sword being near the Adversary's Body, which makes it, more difficult for him to avoid you; besides, by this Parade, you are in better Condition to parry, not only a Thrust below, but also any other Thrusts and Feints, the Sword being near the Situation of Guard.

7th. Plate.

Thrust under the Wrist.

It's Parade.

CHAP. VIII.

Of Quart *under the Wrist.*

This Thrust should not be made but instead of *Seconde,* that is to say, on an Engagement, Parade, or Lunge of the Adversary in *Quart.*

The Wrist must not be so much turned up, nor so high as in *Quart* within; the Body should be more inward, and bending more forward. (Refer to the 7th Plate.)

In case the Adversary pushes *Quart,* in order to take the Time, you must lunge the Foot strong inward, to throw the Body farther from the Line of the Adversary's Sword.

In recovering from this Thrust, the Wrist must be in *Tierce,* and the Sword without the Enemy's whilst the other Parts take their Situation.

The Parade of this Thrust is made by a Half-circle of the Sword within, the Wrist raised in *Quart,* and the Point low. *See the 7th Plate.*

CHAP. IX.

Of Flanconnade.

This Thrust is to be made only in engaging or *risposting* when the Adversary carries his Wrist too far inward, or drops the Feeble of his Sword, then you must press a little within, and with your Feeble on his, in order to lower it, and by that means get an Opening in his Flank.

The Body, in this Thrust, is not so strait as in *Quart* within, tho' the Arms are. *See the 8th* Plate.

It is necessary to oppose with the Left Hand, in order to avoid a low Thrust on your engaging, pushing or *risposting*. This is the last Thrust of the Five which are to be made in our Art. The first us *Quart* within the Sword, the second *Tierce* without the Sword, the third *Seconde* under the Sword, the fourth *Quart* under the Sword, and the fifth, *Flanconnade*; and there is not any Attack, Thrust, Feint, Time or Rispost in this extensive Art, but what depends on one of these.

The Recovery from *Flanconnade*, should be the same as from *Quart* within the Sword.

Flanconnade is generally avoided by taking the Time in *Seconde* with the Body low; the Hand must oppose to shun the Thrust, and hit the Adversary at the same time. Instead of pushing at the Flank, you should push within the Body. *See the 8th* Plate.

Besides the taking Time in *Seconde*, there is another very good Parade, very little practised in Schools; either because few Masters know it, or because it is more difficult to execute it justly. This Parade is made by lowering the Adversary's Sword, bringing it under your's to the Inside, and parrying a little lower on the Feeble of his Sword, you make your *Rispost* where he intended his Thrust, that is to say in the Flank.

8th. Plate.

Flannconade.

The Opposition of the Hand to the lowering the body.

CHAP. X.

Of Parades.

There are two Sorts of Parades, the one by binding the Blade, the other by a dry beat. The binding Parade is to be used when you are to *rispost* in *Quart* within, in *Tierce* without, in *Seconde* under, in *Flanconnade*, and in all *Feints*: And the Beat, giving a favourable Opportunity of *risposting*, is to be used when you *rispost* to a Thrust in *Seconde*; or when after having parryed a Thrust in *Quart* within, you see an Opening under the Wrist. To these two Thrusts, you must *rispost* almost as soon as the adversary pushes, quitting his Blade for that Purpose, which is to be done only by a smart Motion, joining again immediately, in order to be in Defence if the Adversary should thrust.

There are three Things more to be observed in parrying. First, that you are to parry all Thrusts with the inmost Edge, except in yeilding Parades, which are made with the Flat. Secondly, that your Fort be to the Middle, and your Middle to the Feeble of the Adversary's Sword.

And thirdly, that your situation be as rear to the guard as possible, as to favour your riposte.

The ripostes.

In order to riposte well, you must observe the Adversary's Time and Recovery in Guard. The Time is to be taken in the Thrusts of opposition when he is recovering, and the other as soon as you have parryed. There are three ways of riposting on the Adversary's Recovery in Guard: when he does not come enough to the Sword, or not at all: the second, when he comes too much, and the third, when his Recovery and Parade are just. To the first, you must riposte strait; to the second by disengaging, or cutting over or under, according as you see light; and to the last, by making a strait Feint or Half-thrust, to oblige the Adversary to come to the Parade, and then pushing where there is an opening, which is called baulking the parade.

CHAP. XI.

Of the demarches, or manner of advancing and retiring.

Most of the faults committed in making thrusts when the measure is to be closed, proceed from the disorder of the body, occasioned by that of the feet, so that for want of moving well, you are not only in danger of being taken on your time, but likewise you cannot execute your thrusts neatly, justly, nor swiftly; the body being disordered and weak. There are ten demarches in fencing; four in advancing, five in retiring, and one to turn your adversary, or hinder him from turning you. The first demarche in advancing, is made by lifting and carrying your Left-foot the length of your shoe before the right, keeping it turned as in guard, with the knee bent, lifting up the heel of the Right-foot, leaning the body forward, which, on this occasion, gives it more strength and a better air; then carrying the Right-foot about two foot before the left, in order to be in Guard, which is done by a smart Beat of the Right-foot.

The same *Demarche* in retiring, is made by lifting and carrying the Right foot the Length of the Shoe behind the Left, with the Knee a little bent, then carrying the Left-foot on the Line, and to the Distance of Guard.

The second *Demarche* is called closing the Measure; which is done by lifting and advancing the Right-foot a bout a Foot with a Beat, drawing the Left the same Length; because by drawing it more or less you would lose your Strength or your Measure, which few People have observed.

There is such a *Demarche* backward, which is called breaking Measure; which is done by lifting and carrying the Left-foot a Foot back, drawing or bringing back the Right in Proportion according as the Ground will permit.

If the Ground be uneven, or that you have a mind to surprize an unskilful Man by gaining Measure unperceived, or to oblige one, a little expert, to push at the time you advance your Body; you must, I say, if your Adversary is unskilful, bring the Left-foot more or less near the Right, as you are more or less out of Measure, which gains more Ground, and less visibly than the foregoing *Demarche*, and is more favourable to your Thrust: If your Adversary is a little expert, and pushes on this your advancing you must bring back the Left-foot to it's Place, and he will be out of Measure, tho' by Means of his Lunge you will be well in Measure, which is a great Advantage.

The same *Demarche* may be made in retiring, where the Ground is uneven, lifting the Right-foot, bringing it near the Left, and putting back the Left in Guard.

To make a Thrust in three Motions, being out of Measure, you must make a double Beat, which is done by a small Beat of the Right-foot in the same Place, beginning immediately with the same Foot to close the Measure.

The three Ways of retiring which I have shewn, are done from the Situation in Guard. The two which are done after a Lunge are, first by lifting and bringing the Right-foot back from the Place of the Lunge behind the Left, and then carrying the Left behind the Right, in order to be in Guard.

The late Monsieur De Latouche, and Monsieur De Liancour, found this demarche better than the following one, tho' it is not so generally used.

The second Retreat after having pushed, is made by drawing back the Right-foot about the length of the Shoe, bending the Knees, in order to be in a condition to chace or drive back the Left-foot with the Right, keeping the Hams very supple, the Body free, and the Sword before you; not only that you may spring the farther, but also to be in a better Posture of defence. The Point of the Right-foot should come down first, leaning immediately after on the Heel; the Left-foot must fall on the Line at the distance, and in the Situation in Guard, as I before observed, in order to be ready to take the Time, or to make a Riposte.

The two Masters that I have quoted, condemned this Retreat very much, especially Monsieur De Latouche, who says in springing back, three motions are necessary; first to draw back the Right-foot in guard, secondly to bend the Knee, and thirdly to chace or fly back. Any Master, will find that there should be but two motions, it being easy to bend the Knees and draw back the Right-foot at the same Time.

Besides, his rule for springing back is false; for by drawing the Right-foot back so far as in guard; you lose Time, the first Motion being too long, and the Feet being so close together, the Body has not sufficient Strength, and consequently cannot go far. From this it is plain that three Motions are not necessary for springing back, there being but two in all. He likewise says that the leaping back, requires such an effort, that you have not Power to parry; but Experience sufficiently shows that you may easily parry and spring back. Indeed on a moving Sand, or slippery Ground, it is very difficult to leap back; and if we consider things rightly, we cannot find our purpose answered at all times and places; and tho' the first Retreat that I recommended, and which these Gentlemen esteemed, is very good, yet if you are followed closely in retreating thus, as the two Steps do not place you at so great a Distance, by much, as the springing back, you may be put to a Nonplus by a redouble.

When you know the just Length of your Adversary's Thrust, you may break or steal out of measure, by leaning back the Body, without stirring the Foot.

If in the Field, you have the Disadvantage of the Ground, the Wind, or the Sun, or that in a School, you are exposed to too much Light, or, pushing with an awkard Man; in order to obviate these Inconveniencies, you must go round him, which may be done within or without according as you have Room.

The Turning must be done out of Measure, and with great Caution: When 'tis within your Sword, you must begin with your Left-foot, carrying it to that Side, and then bring the Right-foot to it's proper Line and Distance; and if your Adversary turns on the Outside, you must carry the Right-foot to that Side, and the Left in Guard, as well to avoid his Thrusts, as to lay hold on every favourable Opportunity, in case he should persist in his *Demarche*.

You should never give Measure but to your Inferior: Giving Measure, is when the Body and Feet advance too much, or in Disorder; or advancing before you are well situated, although corrected in the *Demarche*, or advancing when you are near enough, except you be much superior to the Enemy.

The Measure should be given to oblige the Adversary to push; in order to get an Opportunity of taking the Time, or of *risposting*.

CHAP. XII.

Of Disengagements.

There is nothing more nice, or more necessary in Fencing, than Disengagements; the nicest Motion, being the smoothest and finest, and the most necessary, there being but few Thrusts where you ought not to disengage, and to several more than once; and there is no better Means of avoiding the Advantage that a strong Man has when he presses on your Sword.

If we confine ourselves, strictly, to the Meaning of Disengagements, we shall find it to be of three Sorts; which are, upon the Blade, over the Point, and under the Wrist: But as this might be too intricate in Lessons, and a Learner mistake one for another; none should be called a Disengagement, but that which is made on the Blade; and though the others are, in effect, Disengagements, especially that over the Point, which is done closer than those under the Wrist, yet they are distinguished from Disengagements, by calling them Cuts over the Point, and under the Wrist, according as they are used.

In order to disengage and push from the Outside to the Inside, being in Guard towards half *Quart*; the Wrist must be raised a little at the Time that you lower the Point and raise it again, which should be done as close as possible, by a smooth and quick Motion, that you may be covered and lose no Time, and be able to push with your Fort to the Adversary's Feeble.

Some People, in pushing *Quart* and *Tierce*, keep the Wrist in *Tierce*, in order to push *Quart* the swifter, which is a Fault; because they accustom themselves to a Situation, which, when they come to assault, is unsafe and dangerous, for want of being in the Guard of Defence.

In disengaging from the Inside to the Outside, the Wrist should turn a little more towards *Quart*, than in the Guard which I have recommended: The Point should fall and rise and the same Instant, and the Hand should turn insensibly in *Tierce*, as the Thrust goes forward.

Some Masters teach to hold the Sword in Guard between *Quart* and *Tierce*, and to disengage in that Situation; whereby the three Advantages which the Disengagement in *Half-Quart* gives you, are lost; that is to say, first, a good Air, secondly, the being covered with the Fort of the Sword, and thirdly, the Swiftness of the Thrust; because the Hand has not a sufficient Freedom of Motion.

The knowing how to disengage barely is not sufficient; it is necessary that you be acquainted with the Time, and with your Adversary's Play, in order to disengage to Advantage. The Time is when the Adversary comes to your Sword; and when your Adversary, depending on his Strength, comes to your Blade, in order to guide his Thrust to your Body, is what is meant by his Play or Manner. You may indeed disengage without taking the Time, but with less Success.

When the Adversary engages swift, 'tis good to keep your Point a little low, or distant from his; by which Means he requires more Time to engage you, and gives you more to prevent him, unless you suffer him to touch your Sword; which would not only make you lose the Time of hitting him, but would also expose you to receive a Thrust, it being certain that when you go to the Blade on one Side, you cannot defend the Other; for you cannot do two opposite Actions at one and the same Time; and by the same Rule, if you miss the Time of disengaging, and disengage too late, you expose yourself to his Thrust; for you cannot, at the same time, quit his Blade and parry.

Though it is necessary that every Fencer should understand the Disengagements, it is more especially so to tall and weak Men. To the first, that they may keep their Adversary at a Distance; which by Reason of their Height, is an Advantage to them; and to the others in order to prevent closing; in which Case, their Weakness would be a Disadvantage to them.

CHAP. XIII.

Of Feints.

Feints are much used in *Fencing*, whether it be by reason of their Number, their Ease, or the Success that attends them, gaining more Time and Light than is to be got in plain Thrusts, there being no Thrust to be given so well as after a Feint.

The Number of Feints is so great, by reason of the many Guards and Parades, that I should find it as difficult to describe them, as the Reader would to comprehend them without Experience; so that I shall confine myself to those from which the rest derive, which are, strait Feint, Feint, and double Feint.

By strait feint, is meant a Motion or Feint to Thrust on the Side on which your Sword is, which is to be done on the Inside, the Wrist in *Quart*, a little higher than the Point which must be near the Adversary's Sword, that you may be covered, whilst you endeavour to get an Opening. This Motion should be attended with a little Beat of the Right-foot, keeping back the Body. If, at the Time you feint, your Adversary does not stir, you must push *Quart*: if he parrys with his Feeble, you must immediately disengage to *Tierce*; and if he parrys high you must cut in *Quart* under the Wrist.

The Feint, to which I give no other Name, it being the most used, and to distinguish it from the others, is done by feinting from *Quart* to *Tierce*, with a little Beat of the Foot, keeping the Body back: the Wrist must be raised in *Quart*, and the Button a little lower than the Pommel, near the adversary's blade; by which means you are covered, and can make your thrust swifter. If the Adversary does not stir at the feint, you must go on strait with the *Tierce*: if he parrys with his Feeble, you must Disengage and thrust *Quart*, and if he parrys with his Fort, you must push *Seconde*.

Several masters teach to make this feint from the inside to the outside, with the Wrist turned in *Tierce*; and indeed they are seemingly in the right; a feint being a likeness of the beginning of a

Thrust; and that likeness cannot be better shown than in the Figure of the Thrust: but the smart motion of the Point, causes the Adversary to stir, the Figure of the Hand no way contributing thereto. You are to consider which is the most proper, not only to make the Adversary answer you, but also to make the Motion quicker. Monsieur De Latouche says, that from *Quart* to *Quart* there is no Motion; but we have two instances to the contrary. First, that a Man of experience has his Wrist and the bend of his Arm free, so as to thrust strait in *Quart*, tho' in the same Figure; and secondly, if there be a Motion preceding the Thrust, as in a Disengagement, or a Cut under; this Motion is sufficient to help the swiftness of the Feint, and of the Thrust: in short, the Motion from *Quart* to *Quart*, being quicker than feinting from *Quart* to *Tierce*, and returning in *Quart*; it ought to have the preference, swiftness being the Line of Fencing. The only Feints that should be made in *Tierce*, are those that are marked from below above to return below, and from above below to return above.

The double feint is in two Motions, so that in order to push within the Sword, you must be without; and making a little Motion in *Quart* within, with a little Beat of the Foot, you feint again without closing the Measure, keeping back the Body in order to be out of the Adversary's Reach: if he parrys with his Fort, you must cut under in *Seconde*, and if he parrys with his Feeble, disengage to *Quart* within.

As there are in this Thrust three motions of the Sword, *viz.* the two Feints and the Thrust; the Foot must make as many, in order to answer the Motions of the Hand.

Some Masters teach to make the double Feint without stirring the Foot; and others teach to advance on the first Motion. In the first Case, being in the Adversary's Measure, you lose too much Time, which is very dangerous: And advancing on the first motion, is almost as dangerous as keeping the Foot firm, by putting yourself within the Adversary's Reach; besides the Manner is not so graceful as that which I recommend, in which you are not within his Reach 'till the second Motion; and this is attended with another Advantage; for by bearing with the Right-foot, the Body must of necessity be kept back, and consequently, farther from the Sword of the Adversary, and in a better Condition to act.

There are two other Ways of making these Thrusts: The one by an Interval between the first and second Motions, joining or uniting the other two; and the latter between the second and third Motions, joining the two first. Though both these Methods are good, I prefer the latter, which puts you in a better Condition, not only to avoid your Adversary's Thrust, but also to chuse your own; the Interval giving you a favourable Opportunity of doing both.

There has been so much said of the Feints which I have described, with their Opposites, that I shall say no more of them, nor will I speak of an infinite Number of other Feints, strait, single, and double, within, without, and under, in disengaging, or cutting over the Point, or under the Wrist, in risposting, or redoubling Thrusts; all which, depend on the three which I have described; in which, as in all Thrusts, the Body must be kept back, and the Fort of the Sword before you; by which Means, you are more out of Danger, and the Wrist is better prepared. Some Men mark Feints with the Head and Body, which is a very disagreeable Sight, and dangerous with Regard to Time.

A Feint is the Likeness of the Beginning of a Thrust: It is made to put the Adversary off his Guard, and to gain an Opening. In order to take Advantage of the Time and Light which you get by your Feint, you must take care to avoid an Inconveniency into which many People fall, by uncovering themselves in endeavouring to uncover the Adversary.

CHAP. XIV.

Of cutting over the Point of the Sword.

In order to cut over the Point, within from without, the Wrist must be turned towards *Tierce*, which gives it a swifter Motion. When your Point is over your Adversary's, you must turn the Wrist in *Quart*, pushing with your Fort to his Feeble: Though this is a regular Way of cutting, what is most essential to perfect the Thrust is wanting, that is to say, the Motion that should precede it, which is commonly a Half-thrust or Feint, by which, two Advantages are gained: First you discompose your Adversary, and secondly, your Thrust is swifter, being by so much the more vigorous, as the Motion previous thereto is so. At the Time you make a Half-thrust or Feint, you must make a little Beat with the Foot, bearing back the Body to break your Adversary's Measure.

The Cut from the Inside to the Outside, has commonly more Success than that from the Outside to the Inside, the Adversary going more readily to his Parade on this Side than on the other. The Manner of cutting on the Outside, is by placing your Sword within, making a little Motion or strait Feint, the Wrist in *Quart*, the Fort of the Sword before you, in order to be covered, and your Point very near the Adversary's Sword; you must beat a little with the Foot, bending the Body back a little, and as the Adversary is going to parry with the Feeble, you must pass your Point quickly over his, pushing in *Tierce*, with your Fort to his Feeble.

Though all Thrusts have the same following Ones; the Cut has them more easy; it's Motion from above to below, disposing it better than the Disengagements, if the Thrust be from the Outside to the Inside, and that the Adversary parrys with his Fort to your Feeble: Besides the Recovery in Guard, which is common after all Thrusts, you must, upon a Parade with the Fort, if it be without stirring the Foot, or in advancing, join: And if the Adversary makes this Parade in retiring, he gives you an Opportunity of cutting in *Quart* under the Wrist, and on his parrying with the Feeble, you must return in *Seconde*, bringing forward the Left-foot a little, in order to procure a Reprise or second Lunge.

These two Reprises are to be made before you are acquainted with your Adversary's Manner of parrying; but when you have discovered it, if it be with his Fort, you must cut over and under the Wrist in *Quart*, and if with his Feeble, return in *Tierce*, that is to say, make an entire Circle. These Cuts are to be made in one or two Motions; in the first you are not to stop, but in the other, you make a short Interval by a little Beat with the Foot.

The Thrusts following the Cut from the Inside to the Outside, before you know your Adversary's Parade, are made thus: If 'tis with the Fort, you must return with a Cut in *Seconde*, under the Sword, advancing the Left-foot a little; If he parrys with the Feeble, you must return by disengaging to *Quart* within, advancing the Left-foot, as before: Some People return a Cut in *Tierce*, in *Quart*, by another Cut over the Point, of *Quart* in *Tierce*, and so on the contrary Side.

When you foresee the Parade, you may at once cut from the Inside to the Outside, and under in *Seconde*; or return within, according as the Parade is made with the Fort or Feeble. You may also make these Redoubles by a little Interval over the Sword, beating with the Foot.

There are other Redoubles which are made by drawing back the Body without stirring the Feet.

See the Chapter of Reprises.

The Cut may be made not only after a Half-thrust, or strait Feint, as I have said, but also after an Engagement, Lunge, or Pass, and in Risposting, which is the best and most used; because that is to be done only in recovering to Guard, or by bringing one Foot behind the other, or springing back; To the first you must Rispost with the Foot firm, and to the other by closing the Measure.

CHAP. XV.

Of the Reprise, *or redoubled Thrust.*

The Term *Reprise* signifies a succession of Thrusts without Interval, or with very little. It may be done in three Manners; First after having pushed without recovering, Secondly, in recovering or being recovered; and Thirdly, when the Enemy steals Measure.

The first and last of these three Reprises may be called Redoubles.

The first Reprise is made after having pushed *Quart*, the Enemy having parryed with his Feeble, you must return in *Seconde*, advancing the left Foot a little to make the Action easier to the right Foot, and tho' it be not necessary to advance it unless the Enemy retires, it serves for an Ornament, and to give more Vigour to the Thrust: But if as soon as the Enemy has parryed he Risposts, you must only redouble with the Hand, the Body low without stirring the Feet, and join. If he Risposts under the Wrist in the Flank, you must either parry crossing his Sword as you recover, opposing with the left Hand, or return, as I said, with the Hand in *Seconde*.

Upon the Rispost of the Enemy, you may also redouble, volting strait, or cutting in the Flank according as he raises his Hand more or less in his Rispost, in order to facilitate your Volt; you must immediately after your Lunge follow a little with the left Foot.

The second Reprise is made, after having pushed *Quarte*, when in recovering to Guard the Enemy advances, without being covered, or that suffering the Superiority of your Sword, he gives you room to thrust in *Quarte*, if he disengages, you must go off in *Tierce*, if he forces your Sword with his Feeble, you must disengage to *Tierce*, and if with his Fort cut *Quarte* under the Wrist.

In order to get time for this Redouble, you must make a half Thrust, immediately getting out of Measure, either with the Body Simply, or by the first Demarche backwards, or by leaping a little back; if the Enemy advances it will be either strait or making a Feint, or on your Sword; to the two first you must push strait *Quarte*, or *Seconde*, lowering the Body or volting, and if he comes on your Sword you must disengage and push over in *Tierce*.

The third Reprise is made when the Enemy upon your pushing *Quarte* breaks Measure without or with parrying; to the one you must redouble in *Quarte*, with your Fort to his Feeble, which is done after a strait Thrust, Feint, Engagement, or Rispost; and if the Enemy parrys, you must likewise redouble forwards by a Disengagement, or a Cut under or over according to his Parade, or as Opportunity offers. To redouble forward, or make several Reprises following with ease, you must as often as you thrust follow with the left Foot.

The Reprises *on the* Outside.

If you push in *Tierce* and your Adversary parrys with the Fort, you must redouble in *Seconde*, and if he parrys with the Feeble disengage to *Quarte*, advancing a little the left Foot that the Right may have the Liberty of a second Motion.

If the Enemy after parrying *Tierce* shou'd Rispost strait or under, to the first you may disengage and volt, and to the other volt strait, advancing the left Foot a little in Lunging, in order to have the Liberty of Volting, because you cannot easily do it when you are extended: It is more easy to take the Time opposing with the left Hand; and 'tis best of all to parry and thrust strait in *Quarte*; if after having pushed *Tierce*, on your Recovery to Guard, you find you have the Command of the Enemy's Sword, or that he advances uncovered, you, must in these Cases push strait in *Tierce* if he disengage you must take the time and push *Quarte*, if he comes to your Sword with his Fort, you must cut under in *Seconde*, if with his Feeble, disengage in *Quarte*, it is also good after having pushed *Tierce* to recover with your Sword high, giving Light under, and if the Enemy pushes there, you must take the Time opposing with the left Hand, or Parry and Rispost.

It is good likewise for a Decoy to make a half Thrust and recover with the Sword quite distant from you Body, and if the Enemy comes to your Sword, you must disengage and thrust at his Open, and if he makes at your Body, you must volt or oppose with the Hand and thrust where you have Light.

The Reprises or Redoubles in advancing are made in *Tierce* by the same Rules as those within are. That is to say, either strait, or by disengaging or cutting over or under, according as the Enemy either lets you make your Thrust, or goes to his Parade.

All these Redoubles may be made on a Rispost as well as on other Lunges.

CHAP. XVI.

Of passing Quarte *within the Sword.*

A Pass is contrary to a Volt as well in Figure as in it's Occasion, the left Leg in the Figure passing foremost, and in a Volt behind, to help the Body to turn, and in it's occasion, the Pass being to be made as in a Lunge, taking the Time, or his Time, whereas the Volt cannot be made without a great deal of Time; yet the Pass is different from a Lunge, the one being made with the foremost Foot, and the Pass with the hindmost, which gives the Thrust a greater Length, more Strength and Swiftness, and a greater Facility of taking the Feeble with your Fort, the Body goes further, because the Center from which it departs in a Lunge is in the left Foot, and in a Pass in the right Foot which is more advanced, and also because in passing you advance the Left Foot more than you do the Right in Lunging, and the Parts being higher on a Pass than in a Lunge there is a greater Facility of taking the Feeble with your Fort.

In a Pass in *Quarte*, the Hands and Arms must be displayed as in a Lunge, not only in their Figure, but in the same Order, that is to say, the Hand must move first to bring on the Shoulder and the Body; which should lean more forward than in Lunging, at the Time that carrying the left Foot about two Foot and an half, you find your Pass at it's full Extention. As your Body is too much abandoned forward to recover itself easily, you must rush on your Enemy, seize the Guard of his Sword, and present him your Point, which is done by advancing the right Foot to such a Distance as to be out of the reach of his Leg whilst you advance, which otherwise might give him an Opportunity, by Tripping to throw you down. As you advance the right Foot you must seize the Guard of his Sword, at the same time drawing back your Sword, keeping it high. Then you must carry your right Foot behind the Left to almost the Distance of a Lunge, in Order to be strong, as well to avoid his pulling you forward, as to draw him to you.

9th. Plate.

A Pass in Quart.

The Lowering the Body on the Pass.

10th. Plate.

The Turning the Body on a Pass in Tierce

Pass in Seconde Volting the Body.

If the Enemy parrys the Pass with his Fort, you must only join, commanding his Sword with your Fort, 'till you have seized his Guard with the left Hand, which must be done at the Time that you advance the right Foot, carrying your Sword from the Inside to the Out, then you must bring the left Foot to the side of the right, and bring back the right presenting the Sword to the Enemy.

If he parrys with his Feeble, you must, without stopping, either cut over his Point from within to without, or turn the Wrist in *Seconde*, lowering your Body, and bringing up the right Foot seize his Guard, then carrying your Sword from within to without, you advance the left Foot to the side of the right, and drawing back the right present your Sword.

The easiest means to avoid and hit a Man who passes in *Quart* within are to parry dry and Rispost swiftly in the Flank, and if the Pass is made straight along the Blade with the Fort to your Feeble, you must by lowering your Feeble, turn your Wrist in *Quarte* carrying the Point perpendicularly down, supporting the Wrist, without, and bringing your Sword round by the Outside of the Adversary's Shoulder, you find your Sword above his, with your Point to his Body. You may also upon the same Pass lower the Body and push *Seconde*.

To Pass in Tierce.

In passing *Tierce*, as in a Lunge, the Wrist must draw the Shoulder and Body forward, bringing, as in a Pass in *Quarte*, the Left-foot about two Feet and an Half before the Right, then advancing the Right foremost and out of the Reach of the Enemy's; you must seize the Guard of his Sword, and again advancing the Left-foot near the Right, you draw back the Right and present the Point.

The Counters or Opposites to this Pass, are the strait Rispost, or the Rispost under, the taking Time, cutting *Seconde* under, disengaging, or counter disengaging and volting, but the surest is to loosen the Right-foot turning the Body half round to the right, opposing with the Sword and presenting the Point to the Enemy, which hindering him from hurting you, throws him on your Point if he abandons himself, and at the same time you seize the Guard of his Sword. *See the 10th* Plate.

To Pass in Seconde.

In passing *Seconde*, there must, as in a Lunge, be a preparatory Motion, which is made by a Feint, or by an Engagement on the Blade to oblige the Enemy to parry high, in order to take that Time to pass under, which is done by advancing the Left-foot very much, with the Body lower and more forward than in other Passes, and advancing the Right-foot, you seize the Enemy's Sword, bringing yours from under over, and advancing the Left-foot to the Side of the Right, you draw back the Right presenting the Point. You must take notice, that in a Pass in *Quarte* with it's Joining, there are but three Steps, and that in the Passes in *Tierce* and *Seconde* there are four. The first, passing the Left-foot before the Right; the second, advancing the Right to seize the Sword; the third, bringing up the Left-foot a little, and the fourth, bringing back the Right, presenting the Point.

In order to avoid, and to hit the Enemy on his Pass, besides parrying and pushing strait, as in the Thrust lunged in *Seconde*, in the 6th Plate, you may also make a strait Thrust, opposing with the Left-hand, or by volting, as is shewn in the Cut of the 10th Plate.

Tho' a Pass carries along with it, as I have observed, a greater Extension and Swiftness than a Lunge, yet as you cannot recover from it, it should be seldom practised, especially if you are not the strongest, or able in three attacks to hit twice, there being nothing more disagreeable to the Sight than to see several Passes made without hitting. But it is otherwise in Lunges, by reason of the Liberty of recovering and parrying.

Passes were more used formerly than they are now, whether it was to endeavour to bring them to Perfection, or because it has been found that this Sort of Play was not so sure.

CHAP. XVII.

Of volting the Body.

The Volting of the Body, which many People call *Quarting*, shou'd never be done but at times when you are abandoned, as in Case of Lunges or on an Engagement of Feint in Disorder, of when finding yourself so disordered as not being able to parry, you must of necessity have recourse to volting in order to avoid the Thrust; but to do it at an improper time, as some do, is very dangerous, by reason of the Facility of parrying it, it being a Figure in Fencing which gives the least Strength, Extention, of Swiftness to a Thrust; besides that presenting the Flank and Small of the Back, the Adversary, in order to hit these Parts, has nothing to do but parry with his point a little within and low.

In volting you must begin with the Arms and Left-foot, by whose Assistance you turn the body; the Hands shou'd turn in *Quarte*, the Right as in a Lunge or Pass, and the Left more without; you must at the same time turn upon the Point of the Right-foot, bringing the Heel outwards, and the Left-foot behind the Right, a little farther outwards, which gives the Body almost the Figure of a Left-handed Man; having turned about a Quarter round, the Body in this Posture must necessarily be in Disorder. *See the 10th Plate.*

Having finished these Motions, if you find, for want of the Enemy's having suficiently abandoned himself, that you have not an Opportunity of Joining, you must without stirring the Body or Left-foot, return with your Sword on the Enemy's, and from his Sword to his Body, and from the Body to the Sword, as often as you shall see proper, which may be easily done, your Thrusts being but of small Extension, as well by reason of the Action of the Enemy coming to you, as by the Advancement of the Volt; you should, at the same time, oppose with the Left-hand, to avoid the Thrusts that the Enemy might make upon the Time of yours; by this means you may easily come to Guard again, or if he retires you may push at him, the Left-foot by it's Advancement having given a great Advantage to your

Thrust, and if instead of retiring, he has a mind to join, you must prevent him by seizing the Guard of his Sword, presenting your Point to him.

If in an Assault the Foil be entangled in the Shirt or elsewhere, or that in Battle the Sword be too far entered, or that the Enemy lay hold on the Blade; in these Cases you must shift your Sword to the other Hand, which is done after the Volt, advancing your Right-foot, taking hold of your Blade with the Left-hand about four inches from the Guard, whilst with the Right you seize his Guard, and drawing back your Sword you present him the Point.

Tho' Volting is not best in Combat, yet it may on some Occasions be necessary, besides it is my Business to speak of them, at the same time advising that 'tis much better to make use of Parades and Risposts, than of Time of what Sort soever.

The Joining on a Volt is the same as on passing in *Quarte*.

CHAP. XVIII.

Of Joining or seizing the Sword.

You may join after having parryed any Thrust or Pass whatever, as also after having pushed, passed, or volted in whatever Figure, or on whatever Side it may be, especially when the Enemy abandons himself, or you abandon yourself: If the Enemy abandons himself by a Lunge or Pass; in case of the first, you must close the Measure in parrying, seizing at the same time the Guard of his Sword with your Left-hand and carrying the Right-foot back present him the Point; and in case of a Pass, you must parry with your Feet firm, and seize his Guard, drawing back the Right-foot and presenting your Point in like Manner.

If you have pushed being too near, that your Right-foot slipped, or that the Enemy in parrying closed Measure; if he parryed with his Feeble you must redouble in *Seconde* and join, and if with his Fort, you must oppose his Sword with your's 'till with your Left-hand you have seized the Guard, advancing the Left-foot; this Motion being done, you pass your Sword over the Enemy's from within to without; and loosing the Right-foot present him your Point.

Upon the Parade of *Tierce* with the Fort, being near you must join, seizing the Guard, advancing the Left Leg, and drawing back the Right, and present the Point; or you may, before you join, cut under in *Seconde*; the first is surer at the Sword, and the other more beautiful in an Assault where a Thrust is more esteemed, than joining.

If on a Pass or Lunge the Enemy shou'd attempt to join or seize your Sword, you must, in order to prevent him, change it from the Right-hand to the Left, four Inches from the Guard, as I have already observed, seizing his with the Right-hand, and presenting him the Point, holding it at such a Length as to hit him whilst he is unable to come near you.

11th. Plate.

The Seizing and presenting the Sword.

Parrying and Disarming.

In Joining, if you cannot seize the Guard, you must the Blade, helping with your Elbow, turning the Hand to break the Blade, or take away the sword, which may be done if you are cunning and nervous, especially if the Enemy's Wrist is in *Quarte*, in which there is no Danger of hurting yourself, because the Sword cannot slip thro', and consequently, can't cut your Fingers, as has happened to some by their Imprudence; by this Means, you have time not only to secure yourself, but also to hit your Enemy. Some People seize the Arm, but that is of no use, because the Enemy may change Hands and hit you.

You may throw a Man down after having pushed, either upon the Pass of *Quarte* or *Tierce*; if in *Quarte*, it is done after advancing the Left-foot, crossing the Enemy's Sword with your Fort, and carrying your Right-Leg without his, at the same time pushing the Sword up from the Inside to the Out, and carrying the Right Arm to his Neck, and the Left to the Small of his Back: These three Actions must be done at the same time. There has been so much said on this Head, with the Joining without, that I shall say no more of it.

The Joining in Passes within, without, and under, is the same as in their Lunges.

In whatever Manner you join you must present the Sword at a Distance, in order to hinder the Enemy from seizing it, or putting it off with his Left Hand to throw himself in upon you: If the Enemy shou'd make a Difficulty of yeilding up his Sword, you must, in order to frustrate his Hopes of closing you, and to make him follow you, draw back the Left-foot behind the Right, and the Right behind the Left, at such a Distance as to be strong, at the same time moving the Point of your Sword circularly; by this Means, you are in a Condition either of giving or taking his Life, which you would not be if he could close you, by which you would be oblig'd to kill him, or render the Advantage doubtful by struggling.

CHAP. XIX.

Of engaging in Quarte *in a midling Guard.*

I Have hitherto treated of the Means whereby to make Thrusts, and in this and the following Chapters, I will shew on what Occasion they are to be made use of. Tho' there is an infinite Number of Figures or Postures, and that every Posture may be in Guard, whether within, or without, *Prime, Seconde, Tierce,* or *Quarte,* they proceed from the Midling Guard, the Strait, the High, or the Low Guard, each of which may be attacked and defended within or without.

Though there are many Means to disorder the Enemy by putting him out of Guard in order to hit him on that Occasion, they all depend either upon a Feint by the Side of his Sword to draw him on, or on a Motion of your Sword on his, to uncover him, taking his Sword from the Line of your Body, and placing yours on a Line with his, which is called engaging. And there are several other Ways of coming to the Sword, which are the Beats, Crossings, Bindings, and Lashings; the Occasions of which, and the Manners of using them, I shall shew in their proper Places. I begin with engaging in the midling Guard, as the neatest, the most used, and the best.

To engage this Guard within, it must be done with the Edge on the same Side, without going wide, in order to keep your Fort before you, and your Point before the Enemy, carrying both Parts alike; the Engagement must be made Feeble to Feeble, a little more to your Enemy's than your own, because if it were with the Feeble to the Fort, the Enemy's Sword would not be displaced, besides if he should push, you could not parry, being unable with your Feeble to resist his Fort; and if it were with the Fort to the Feeble, you wou'd be in Danger of being hit under, where there would be an Opening; besides you would be oblig'd to advance much, which would be dangerous.

On your Engagement, the Enemy may do Three things, either of which, produces several others. First, either he will let you engage, or secondly, he will disengage, or thirdly, he will come to your Blade.

If he lets you engage, you must push *Quarte*, or, by way of Precaution, make a Half-thrust, in order to see if he stirs, to retire, or to have recourse to his Parade, or to Time.

If he does not stir, you must, as I said, push *Quarte*; if he retires, redouble your Thrust; if he parrys with his Fort cut *Quarte* under the Wrist; if with the Feeble, disengage, or cut over the Point in *Tierce*; and if upon the Half-thrust he takes the Time pushing strait, you must parry and risposte, or take the Time in *Seconde*, with your Body low; if he takes the Time lowering his Body, you must parry and oppose with the Left-hand, risposting in *Quarte*; if he takes the Time cutting under the Wrist, you must parry crossing the Sword in *Quarte*, opposing with the Hand, in order to make your Rispost more safely; and if he volts upon the Half-thrust, you must parry and risposte in *Flanconnade*, or take the Time, with, your Body low.

If when you engage he disengages, it will be either, 1st, without Design, or 2dly, to disengage and push *Tierce* over, or 3dly, disengage breaking Measure, or 4thly, disengage, and come to your Blade without, or 5thly disengage making a Feint, and pushing *Quarte* or 6thly, disengage to take a Counter to your Time.

- 1st. If he disengages with a Design only to disengage, you must on the Time push *Tierce*.

- 2dly. If he disengages breaking Measure, you must redouble in *Tierce*, advancing.

- 3dly. If he disengages and pushes without, you must parry and risposte quick where you have Light, or take Time against him, disengaging and volting, or lowering the Body.

- 4thly. If he disengages and comes to your Blade without; if 'tis with his Fort, you must cut under in *Seconde*; and if with the Feeble, you must Counter-disengage from without to within.

- 5thly. If on the Engagement, he feint *Tierce* in order to push *Quarte*, you must push or take the Time strait upon the Feint, or by lowering the Body on the Thrust.

- 6thly. If he disengages giving Light, to take a Counter to your Thrust, whether by a Rispost or Time, you must make a False-time or Half-thrust, and if he parrys, or takes the Time, in Case of the first, you must baulk his Parade; and if he takes the Time, you must take another upon him.

If, upon the Engagement, he goes to your Blade with his Fort, you must cut under his Wrist, and if with his Feeble, disengage and push without in *Tierce*.

Though an Engagement may be made Blade to Blade, without Disengaging, that is Inside to Inside; better and more common to make it by disengaging from the Outside to the Inside.

CHAP. XX.

Of engaging in Tierce *in the Midling Guard.*

The Engagement without shou'd be made from your being placed within, Feeble to Feeble, for the same Reason as in *Quarte*, the Wrist shou'd be turned in *Tierce*; in this Engagement as in *Quarte*, the Antagonist may do three things. 1st, let you engage him, 2d. or disengage, 3d. or come to your Blade.

If he lets you engage him, you must carry on your Thrust in *Tierce*, or make a Half-Thrust, to see if he does not stir, if he retires, if he parrys, or if he takes the Time.

If upon your Half-thrust he does not stir, you must thrust strait, if he retires, advance and redouble.

If he parrys with his Fort, cut *Seconde* under, if with his Feeble, you must disengage or cut over the Point from *Tierce* to *Quarte*, and if upon the Half-thrust he takes the Time pushing strait, you must either parry and risposte, or make him Time, volting or lowering the Body.

If he takes the Time in *Seconde*, lowering his Body, you must either parry him and thrust *Quarte*, or pushing *Quarte*, oppose with the Left hand, or volt.

If on your Engagement he disengages, 'tis as in *Quarte*, 1st either without Design, 2d. or to retire, 3d. or to take the Time pushing *Quarte* or volting, 4th. or to come to your Blade, 5th. or to make a Feint; 6th. or to take a Counter to your Thrust.

- 1st. If he disengage without Design, you must push strait in *Quarte*, or make a Half-thrust, and go on with the same.

- 2d. If he disengages breaking Measure, you must come forward redoubling in Quarte.

- 3d. If he disengages and pushes Quarte, which, on this Occasion, is called Counter-disengaging, you must either parry and risposte, or take the Time lowering the Body, or volting.

- 4th. If he disengages and comes to your Sword within, with his Fort, you must cut Quarte under the Wrist, and if with his Feeble, you must Counter-disengage from the Inside to the Outside.

- 5th. If he makes a Feint in order to return in Tierce, you must either parry or take the Time as I have said.

- 6th. If he disengages giving Light, to take a Counter on your Thrust, whether by Rispost or Time, you must make a Feint, and if he parrys with his Fort you must cut under in Seconde, if with his Feeble, you must disengage and push Quarte, if he takes the Time strait, you must lower the body, if he takes Time lowering his body, you must parry and push strait in Quarte, if he cuts in Flank, you must parry crossing the Sword in Quarte, and if he volts, you must parry and risposte in Flanconnade.

If on the Engagement without, he comes to your Sword with his Fort, you must cut under in *Seconde*, if with his Feeble, disengage or cut over the Point in *Quarte*.

When you are engaged within the Sword.

If the Enemy engage you within with his Fort, you must cut under the Wrist, and if with his Feeble, disengage from within to without, of if you don't care to do that, make a Feint without; if on this Feint he goes to the Parade with his Fort, you must push *Seconde* under, and if with his Feeble, disengage in *Quarte*.

When the Enemy engages to make you push, in order to parry and rispost, you must, as I have said, make a Half-thrust and retire giving Light, in order to take him by a Counter to his thrust, by a Parade, or by Time.

You may on the same Engagement, remain engaged on purpose, in order to make the Adversary path strait; and in this Case, you must parry and risposte where he is uncovered, or take Time lowering the Body.

If after having engaged you he shou'd make a Feint, you must, by going to the Parade, give Light on purpose, and if he pushes, take him by a Contrary.

If he engages to make you disengage, in order to take the Time on your Disengagement, you must disengage and give him a little Light, and if he pushes at it, take him by a Rispost, or a Time opposite to his.

If you are engaged in *Tierce* with the Fort, you must cut under the Wrist in *Seconde*, and if with the Feeble, and the Hand in *Quarte*, disengage to *Quarte* within, or, by Way of Caution, make a Half-thrust; if the Adversary goes to the Parade, you must push where you have Light, and if he takes the Time, parry and risposte, or take a Time to his.

You may also upon an Engagement in *Tierce*, make a Feint below, and if he takes the Time, parry above and risposte below. This Thrust is very good against a Man that's disorder'd, who coming to the Parade above, gives room to hit him below.

CHAP. XXI.

Of several Guards, and the Manner of attacking them.

Tho' all the Guards are Good when well defended, yet they are not equally good; because we ought not to look upon any thing as good, that does not procure us some Advantage, and an ill placed Guard, instead of being favourable, requires a great deal of Skill to be of any Use at all, being farther from a Posture of Defence, the midling Guard only carrying with it such a Disposition of the Point and Wrist as is sufficient to defend the Inside, the Outside, the Upper and Lower Parts of the Body with the Sword: For as to the other Guards, whether Flat, High, or Low, or holding the Sword with both Hands, they leave some Part uncovered, either by reason of their Height, or their Line.

To attack a strait Guard.

No Man of Skill or Reason will give a considerable Open without a Design, and as the People who hold such a Guard as I am going to describe, have their several Designs, you must be cautious of them, in order not only to make them useless to them, but advantageous to yourself.

Some Men hold their Swords strait or flat,[3] whether 'tis because they are more used to Disengagements than Parades, or to take Advantage of the Superiority of their Stature, or of the Length of their Sword, to avoid the Attacks and Engagements to which the other Guards are more exposed; for you can hardly engage or feint on this Guard, the Point being too low; so that to attack him, you must bind the Sword, which you must do after placing yourself within his Sword, binding his Blade under yours, when he is out of Measure, to take, with more Ease, the Feeble of his Sword, crossing it with yours, raising your Hand in *Seconde*, and carrying the Point low, whilst gaining Measure, you form a little Circle with the two

Points, and raising them up again, you push *Seconde* within, with the Body low.

Tho' it be almost impossible for the Enemy to disengage, when you have bound his Sword as I have described, it may happen that if some of the Circumstances were wanting, he might disengage and push, which ought not to hinder you from making your Thrust; because your Sword may very well hit him, passing under his, which cannot hurt you, because of the Lowness of your Body.

The Binding is easy to be parryed, by reason of the natural Tendency to follow the Sword, which is done by raising and bringing your Fort nearer. These following have commonly more Success.

The first is made after having bound the Sword, instead of pushing *Seconde* within, you must, upon the Parade, disengage and push *Tierce* over: If the Adversary is quick enough in his Parade to shun this double Motion, you must have recourse to the third, binding the Sword in the like Manner, and feinting above, return below.

Tho' the Sword is seldom bound on the Outside, upon some Occasions and to some People it would not be amiss; it must be done with your Feeble to the Enemy's, with the Precautions necessary in binding within, by a little Circle without, the Hand in *Quarte*, and if he does not stir, or if he disengages, you must push without, the Hand in *Quarte*. These following are according to the Parade with the Fort or with the Feeble, pushing *Seconde* under, or *Quarte* within.

As in all Thrusts the Hand must be easy and uniform, it must be more so in this than in the others, because the Binding cannot be made without a very close and smooth Motion.

Though several Masters teach to disengage in order to bind the Sword, I would not have it done so for two Reasons: First, because the disengaging gives Time to the Opponent, not only to thrust strait, but also to disengage; and Secondly, because you cannot so easily bind the Sword as when you are on the same Side.

In binding the Blade, you must close the Measure; because a Man who is superior to you, in Height, by the Length of his Sword, or by

12th. Plate.

Attack in the high Guard.

Attack in the low Guard.

his Situation, won't let his Inferior into Measure; in one or the other Case, being at a proper Distance, you bind more easily on the Feeble.

To attack the high Guard.

In this Guard, you must place yourself under, with the Hand in *Seconde*, covering the upper Part, in order to oblige the Enemy to go under; which being the most distant Place from his Sword, procures you more Time to avoid him. He may, on this Occasion, do three things: Let you engage him, go under, or force your Sword.

If he lets you engage him, 'tis either with a Design to parry, or to take the Time; wherefore, before you push, you must make a Half-thrust under: If he parrys, it will be in one of the three Ways that I have shewn in the Parade of *Seconde*, Chap. 8, where you may see all their Counters.

If upon the Half-thrust he takes the Time, you must parry and risposte below, or push strait, opposing with the Hand; you may also volt on this Occasion, but it is better to parry.

If he opposes with his Hand upon your Half-thrust, you must parry with your Left-hand, and, pushing near his Left Shoulder, baulk his Hand.

And if he volts on your Half-thrust, you must parry and risposte in the Flank.

If on the Engagement he thrust under, you must parry and thrust strait, or take the Time, opposing with your Hand, and if instead of going under, he only feints there in order to return above; you must either parry the Feint and risposte under, or push on the time, as I have said before.

If he makes use of the same Thrust, pushing at the Time of your going under, you must make believe to push there, returning quickly to the Parade above, and risposte under.

And if he would draw you on in order to make this Rispost on you, you must make a Half-thrust, keeping on your Parade below, to risposte strait in *Quarte*.

If upon your Engagement he forces your Sword, you must yeild the Feeble, opposing with the Fort and the Left-hand. *See the 5th* Plate.

To keep the Enemy from forcing your Sword, you must cross his Blade with your Fort to his Feeble.

To attack the low Guard.

Those who hold a low Guard have a Design either to parry with the Sword or with the Hand, to lower the Body or to volt; therefore as in the other Guards you must make a false Time, or half Thrust, and if he parrys with the Sword, thrust where you see Light, if he parry with the Hand, you must feign a strait Thrust in order to bring his Left-hand to the Parade, at the same time raising your Point with a little Circle, pushing at the left Side with the Hand in *Seconde*, the Body low, whereby you baulk his Left-hand, and for the greater Safety, you must oppose his Thrust with your Hand, endeavouring in your Risposts, to deceive his Sword and his Hand.

If he waits for your Thrust in order to lower the Body or to volt, you must make a Half-thrust to draw him on, and take one of the Counters which I have spoken of before.

If the low Guard is within your Sword, you must attack it making a Semi-circle with the Point of the Sword down, lashing and crossing his, the Hand in *Quarte*, and to push without Danger, you must oppose with the Left-hand: This Thrust is good against a Man that pushes at the same Time.

If the low Guard is without your Sword, you must lash in *Tierce*, crossing the Sword and push without.

If the low Guard is neither within nor without, you must lash smartly in *Tierce* and in *Quarte*, that is to say on his Outside and Inside, pushing *Quarte* afterwards, opposing with the Left-hand: This Thrust puzzles a Man who disengages quick, which in this Case is of no use.

You may also engage this Guard placing yourself within, the Wrist in *Tierce*, and the Point low[4] closing the Enemy pretty near to oblige him to push above, and if he pushes there, you must parry and riposte above, or under, according as you have Light.

If instead of making a Thrust above, he makes a Feint there and pushes within, or under, you must push *Quarte*, opposing with the Left-hand, or else going to the Parade with the Sword to all Thrusts and Feints without, leave to the Left-hand the Defense of the Inside, and of the under Part.

And if instead of pushing, he waits for your Thrust to take the Time upon it, you must press close upon him and push strait in *Quarte*, with the Point low, opposing with the Left hand, in order to throw off his Sword, or push at his Arm, of which you are in Reach, though he is not in Measure of your Body.

These Sorts of Guards are not so much practised, with Sword in Hand, as the middling Guard, People being more careful of parrying with the Sword, and a Man is in much better Condition to parry from the middling Guard than from any other.

To attack the Guard where the Sword is held in both Hands.

Those who hold the Sword in both Hands, that is to say, the Handle in the Right-hand, and the Blade about four Fingers Breadth in the Left, will either engage, or beat on your Sword, with great Force, or stick to a strong Parade, in order to uncover you the more, in Favour of their Thrust.

But as they cannot keep this Situation without exposing their Body very much, which is often dangerous, as also a very unseemly Posture, this Guard is therefore, with good Reason, condemned by most, if not all, experience'd Masters.

If you have to do with one that holds this Guard, you must keep your Point a little low, and be always ready to change, in order to render the Strength which the Left-hand gives to the Right, useless, in his engaging or beating.

If he will not attack you, but waits for your Thrust in order to parry and riposte, you must make a Half-thrust, and recover quickly to your Parade, to avoid his Rispost; wherein, throwing back his Left-hand, and abandoning himself extremely, he is not in a Condition to avoid your Thrust after you have parryed his.

You may also make a Home-thrust on him, by a single or double Feint, because these require two or three Parades; so that your Adversary being unable to parry without throwing his Point a great way off, he cannot bring it back in time if you disorder him by a Feint.

You may likewise catch him, by placing your Sword along his, with your Point a little raised, and sliding on a Defence along his Sword, push at his Left-hand or Arm, for he cannot, tho' he goes to his Parade, hinder your Blade from sliding so as to hit him there, without running any Risque, you being in Measure of his Hand and Arm, when he is out of Reach of your Body.

You are to observe, that in all Guards with Sword in Hand, you must push at the nearest and most uncovered Part; which in the Guards that I have described is the Arm; therefore you must not abandon yourself to hit the Body, but in risposting, or after having disordered, or engaged the Enemy as aforesaid.

CHAP. XXII.

Of Left-handed Men.

Most People imagine that a Left-handed Man has, by Nature, the Advantage of a Right-handed Man in Fencing, whereas he has it only by Habit, exercising oftener with Right-handed Men than a Right-handed Man with him, as well in Lessons as in Assaults, most Masters being Right-handed, as well as most of the Scholars, taking Lessons from the Right-hand, and practising seldom with Left-handed Men, find themselves puzzled, nothing surprizing more than what one is not used to, which is so true, that to embarrass a Left-handed Man, who has not fenced much, you must put another against him; I say one that has not fenced much, because Right or Left-handed Men who go to the School of a perfect Master, will be taught to use both Hands, by which Means, they will not be so much surprized when they meet with a Left-handed Man, as they would otherwise be.

When a Right and a Left-handed Man fence together, the Right handed Man should push but seldom within, that being the Antagonist's strongest Part; and his weakest and outward, which should be kept covered, or in a defensive Condition, as the most liable to be attacked; the best Way is to push *Quarte* without, Engagements, Feints under, and Thrusts above, and double Feints, finished above or under the Wrist in *Quarte*, Cuts over the Point without, and upon the Parade, with the Fort, or with the Feeble, redoubling *Quarte* under the Wrist, or *Seconde* over: These are chiefly the Thrusts which a Right-handed and a Left-handed Man may make against each other, whether on an Attack, or in Defence, by Time or Risposts.

Several Masters puzzle their Scholars by telling them that with a Left-handed Man they must act quite contrary to what they do with a Right-handed, which appears to be false; because to a Right or Left-handed Man you must push, opposing with the Sword, which is to be done by pushing *Quarte*, when the Enemy is within your Sword, and *Tierce*, when he is without. All the Difference between a Right and a Left-handed Man is, that two Right, or two Left-handed Men, are both within or without, whereas a Right with a Left-handed Man, the one is within when the other is without, the one in *Quarte*, the other in *Tierce*.

CHAP. XXIII.

Of the Parade of the Hand.

There are, in Fencing, three Parades with the Left-hand: The first, like the Opposition that is from the Top to the Bottom; the second, with the Palm of the Hand without, towards the Right Shoulder, and the third, from the Bottom to the Top, with the Outside of the Hand: Of these three Parades, the first is the easiest, the most used, and the least dangerous: They are condemned by able Men, as weakening those of the Sword; wherefore it is wrong in a Master to shew them to a Scholar, before he has practised those of the Blade a good while, which being longer, can return to all feints, which the Left-hand cannot, it being impossible to parry with it except you be near, which is very dangerous, as well by reason of the Difficulty of meeting properly with the Sword, as of the Facility of deceiving the Hand, which in this Case has not Time to come to the Parade, because of it's small Distance; and besides the Facility of deceiving it, you need only push at the Arm, Sword in Hand, in order to make it useless.

Of the Opposition of the Hand.

Many People make no Distinction between the Parade and Opposition of the Hand, tho' there is a very great Difference, the Parade being made only against the Adversary's Thrust, and the Opposition to prevent a following Thrust after having parryed with the Sword, which is very necessary in most Thrusts, especially in the Risposts which may be made to your Thrust in *Seconde.*

Besides the Opposition of the Hand, after having parryed with the Sword, you may oppose with it, taking the Time, that is to say, when the Enemy pushes from above to below, as the motion of his sword is greater than your's, having only a strait line to push *Quarte* on, whereas his from above to below, is crooked, so that pushing upon his time, he cannot avoid the thrust, and you may easily oppose his with the Left-hand, which is very different from the parade with the Hand, to which you do not push 'till after you have parryed.

CHAP. XXIV.

Of the beat of the Foot, in closing the measure, or in the same place.

Though it may seem to many people, that the beat of the Foot, in gaining measure, making appels, or alurements, engagements, or other Thrusts, is rather ornamental than necessary; nevertheless, there is nothing puts the Foot in a better condition to follow the swiftness of the Wrist, in most of the actions of the Sword; nor can any thing contribute more to the equal situation, and to the retention of the Body, qualities, which keeping you covered from the time of your combatant, procures you the means, not only of taking advantage of his, but also of possessing firmness, freedom, justness and swiftness. You are to observe two sorts of beating, the one with the Foot firm in the same place, the other gaining measure; the Beat with the Foot firm, is done in two ways, the one in appels, or alurements on the Blade, and the other in engagements or Feints. That upon the allurement on the Blade, may be made by a single beat of the Foot, but those who are pretty well advanced, make two without lifting the Foot but once, the first with the Point, and the other with the whole Foot: that on engagements or single Feints, shou'd have but one beat, the thrust being to be made on the second motion. The beat of the Foot in marching or advancing, is also divided into two sorts, the one in Engagements or single Feints, and the other in Engagements and Feints following, or in double Feints; the manner of engaging must be with a single beat gaining measure, and that of engaging with a double Feint, must be done with a double beat, in order to agree with the motion of the Wrist; and as in all, including the lunge, there must be three beats; you must, on the First Time or Feint, beat with the whole Foot in the same Place, at the second Motion of the Wrist beat again with the foot getting Measure, and at the third Motion push.

You must observe, that between the first and second Motion, there is no Interval, but between the second and third there is, in order to see where the Enemy gives Light: This Interval must be shorter or longer according as your Disposition or Practice is more or less.

CHAP. XXV.

Of the Good Effects of a nice Discernment of the Eye.

In Fencing, there is the Foreseen, and the Unforeseen; the Foreseen is the Effect of the Understanding and of the Will, and the Unforeseen is the Effect of the Discernment of the Eye, and of Custom; which being upheld by this Quality, has no sooner discerned an Action or Opening of the Enemy, than all the Parts which are to act, display themselves to oppose or attack him, as if they depended on the Eye. To be convinced of this Truth, you may reflect on READING, wherein, as soon as the Eye has discerned the Words, the pronouncing them follows as quick as in a studied Discourse; the Eye and Tongue being so disposed by Custom, as to do it without immediately reflecting. Indeed before they cou'd arrive to this, the Understanding and the Will were necessary, which having been united for a certain Time, have communicated such a Habit to these Parts, as to make them act as it were of themselves.

In order to acquire this Quality in Fencing, it is necessary that the Master, in his Lessons, shou'd shew what Opportunities are to be favourably laid hold of, two opposite Actions at one and the same Time, That whilst he is uncovering some Part of his Body, he cannot, at the same Instant, parry, because by the Parade, it must be covered; so that by making them make their Thrusts, and other Motions, by the Discernment of the Eye, they find themselves by Practice ready to oppose all the Motions of the Antagonist without the Assistance of the Will. This Method is indeed a little more tedious in the Beginning, but it afterwards becomes shorter and more certain.

If you have not had Practice enough to make the Discernment of the Eye thus habitual, you must observe what Motions your Action causes in the Adversary, by making a Half, or Home-thrust, in order to discover whether the Enemy has recourse to the Parade, or to the Time: If he goes to parry, you must observe his Manner, in order to make a Feint resembling the same Thrust, and to push at the Part where you observed him to give the Light; and if he goes to the

Time, you also make a Feint, preparing yourself for the parade and Rispost, or to take a Time contrary to his.

CHAP. XXVI.

Of Time.

If we were to follow the exact Term of Time, every Thing that is done in Fencing might be called so; for you shou'd never thrust but when you have a favourable Opportunity of hitting, nor parry, but at the Time that favours you to oppose the Enemy's Sword, not make an Engagement, nor a Feint, but to take the Time upon the Motion that your Action occasions in the Adversary.

Time is the Duration of any Motion: It is called Time because it is the most favourable Opportunity of pushing, the Enemy being unable during one Action to do a contrary one.

It is divided into several Manners and Terms: The first is called the Time, the second, taking his Time, the third, Time to Time, the fourth, the same Time, and the fifth, false Time.

1. Taking the Time, is making your Thrust by a judicious Discernment on the Motion of the Enemy, taking him by a contrary one: You are to know that every Motion, of whatever Part it be, is called Time; for which Reason, I shall say nothing of Feints, Engagements, and Disengagements, upon which it may be taken; and that in three Manners, viz. strait, lowering the Body, or volting it, which you must know how to apply. In a strait Thrust the Time shou'd be taken by lowering and volting the Body, because the Thrust coming strait, if you were to push the same Way, you would, by supporting the Wrist, make a Contrast; and by pushing crooked, you would make a Coup Fourrés, or an interchanged Thrust; but if the Thrust be in Two Times, or Motions, you may push on the first; If it be in three Motions, on the second. As to the volting and lowering the Body, they may be used on all Motions, provided they be abandoned, and that the Enemy does not keep back his Body to drawyou on.

2.   Taking his Time, is the most subtle Thing in Fencing, depending principally on the Mind: The Manner of taking it proceeds from your Place or Situation, which gives you an opportunity of knowing the fort and the feeble of the enemy, so that feeling his blade with your's, you may by a judicious custom, push at a proper instant, according as you find the weakness of his sword; and though it may seem that the enemy, in the same guard, and at the same distance, can as easily parry; that does not happen because of his different design to push, disengage, or make a feint, by reason of the several operations of the mind which follow the will.

3.   The Time to Time, or the Counter to Time, is by several people, called Counter-time: this cannot in effect alter this necessary part of the art; it being but an impropriety in terms; when they say that making a motion to bring the Enemy on, and when he is going to make a Thrust, the making a Counter; this is by consequence a Counter Time, like a Counter-disengagement, without observing that a Counter-time is nothing but an ill timed Motion, which should upon all occasions be avoided: and if that argument were to take place, it might be said that there is no such thing in fencing as taking the Time, because it is to be done only by taking a Time contrary to that which is intended to be taken of you, which according to their Argument would be a Counter-time; whereas the Term Time to Time, or counter to Time, sufficiently shews, that it requires three Motions; since the taking the Time requires two, and the taking it at the Time that he takes it, must require a third. Of these three Motions you are to make two: The first, in order to get one from the Enemy, that you may have an Advantage by your second, which is the third Time; so that when he thinks to take the Time upon you, you take it upon him, which, far from being a Counter-time, is a Time to his, or Counter to his Time.

4.   The same Time, depends on three Things: First, that both having a Design to push, you both push by chance at once, without expecting it from each other: Secondly: That full of

the Design to take the Time, and not knowing it, you push upon the Enemy's Thrust, without foreseeing how to avoid it; and thirdly, when an Inferior or desperate Man, unable to defend himself, had rather run on your Thrust in endeavouring to hit you, than strive in vain to avoid it. These are not only the Occasions of the same Time, but also of the Coups Fourrés.

It is to be observed, that Time, and the same Time, differ only in their Figure, and not in their Occasion, as Monsieur De la Touche says, for to take the Time upon a Thrust, you must go off upon the Lunge, as if it were on the same Time, except that the Figure of the Body shuns the Thrust, which in that of the same Time it does not do.

5.   False Time, is a Motion made by the Enemy to draw you on, in order to take a Time upon your's; therefore he that would take the Time, shou'd distinguish whether the Motion made, is to disorder him, and take the Advantage of his Parade, or to make him thrust, and take the Advantage of his Lunge; In Case of the first, it would be a Fault not to push; and in Case of the other, it would be amiss to push. Some Masters call the false Time, Half Time, which is wrong, every Motion being a Time, and as it is impossible to make a Half Motion, so 'tis impossible to make a Half Time.

The Difference of Time between the dexterous and awkard is, that the dexterous present and take the Time, and the others, give and lose it.

CHAP. XXVII.

Of Swiftness.

Swiftness is the Shortness of Time between the Beginning and End of a Motion: It proceeds from a regular and frequent Exercise, joined with a good Disposition; that is to say, Vigour and Suppleness, which form Agility.

A great Swiftness cannot be acquired without long Practice and a good Disposition, the one not being sufficient, without the other, to give it: For the best natural Parts, without Practice, will be of very little Service to those who have the best Disposition; and the most regular Practice without the Assistance of Nature, will never make a Man perfectly Swift.

Swiftness in Fencing, is so necessary, that without this Quality, it is very difficult to defend, and impossible to offend: This Truth is so well known, that every one is earnestly desirous of it, tho' most People are ignorant of the Means necessary to acquire it.

What contributes most to the becoming swift, besides, frequent Exercise and a fine Disposition, is a perfect Situation of the Parts, the Retention of the Body, and the regular Motion of the Wrist: The Situation requires this advantageous Point of all the Parts, to communicate Freedom and Vigour to the Action, that they may act with Quickness. In order to retain the Body, it is necessary that it be always in it's perfect Situation, during the Motions previous to the Thrust; and if the Thrust consist of one Time only, the Wrist must begin.

As to the Motion of the Hand, it must not only be animated, but also the Action must not be wide, whether in Disengagements, Engagements, Feints, or Risposts; because if you would be soon at your Mark, it is not sufficient to go quick, but it is also necessary that the Action be close.

Many People have confounded the Swiftness of pushing with precipitate or consecutive Thrusts, without considering that Precipitation is either when the Body moves before the Hand, or when an improper Motion is made; and the consecutive Thrusts, the pushing several Times without Interval, or when there is no Occasion; which may be done by one who is not swift; for Swiftness is only the Shortness of Time between the Beginning and End of an Action, as I have already said.

Swiftness and Time are very justly called the Soul of Fencing, and all Thrusts owe their Success to these Qualities; for you cannot hit but by Surprize, nor surprize but by Swiftness.

There are three Ways of surprizing in Fencing: The first is the Situation of the Guard, taking his Time: The second, is doing an Action to disorder the Enemy, in order to hit him, at that Time, where he is open; and the third is when the Opponent attacks you, either by Feints, Engagements, or Lunges, you take him upon the Time. Tho' these three Sorts of Surprize require a certain Point of Swiftness, the first needs the most, having no other Support; but the two others have the Advantage of having disorder'd the Enemy.

Although Time, Swiftness, and the other Qualities are absolutely necessary in Fencing, without their just Concurrence they are useless. In order to acquire which, the Wrist must be easy by Practice, that you may hit where you see Light.

CHAP. XXVIII.

Of Measure.

Time, Swiftness, and Justness, without the Knowledge of Measure, would be in vain, Thrusts from afar being of no Use, and from near, dangerous; and the other Motions shou'd also be at a certain Distance, in order not only to be ready for the Time, but also to take Advantage of the Disorder of the Enemy. The Measure is taken from you to the Enemy, and from the Enemy to you: The first is easier known, as well because it is naturally so, as by the Custom of your Lunge, which being, in regard of yourself, always the same, makes it easier by Practice: The Measure from the Enemy to you is difficult, from the Difference in Persons whose Stature, Activity, or Swords, are not always alike; and tho' the Height shou'd be the same, the Arms, Thighs and Legs are not proportionable; besides there are big Men that have short Arms, and little Men that have long Arms. It is likewise so in regard to the Clift; some being longer in the Fork than others; and though two Men shou'd in that Particular be alike, if one of them has shorter Legs than the other, he will reach farther, because his Thighs are longer, and in the Lunge, only one of the Legs contributes to it's Length, the other making a Line almost perpendicular, whereas the two Thighs making a strait Line, contribute equally to the Extention.

The Difference in Suppleness, also makes a Difference in the Extention; a Man who has the Freedom of his Shoulders and Hips, going farther than one that has them constrain'd. It may also happen that two Men of like Proportion and Freedom of Parts, may not have an equal Extention, by their being taught differently; some Masters teaching to keep the Body upright, the Wrist raised, or too much on one Side, and the Left-foot first; whereas the Body shou'd lean a little forward, without raising or carrying the Hand to one Side, farther than to keep the Body covered, and the Left-foot shou'd lye down on the Edge; this Situation gives a greater Length than the other.

The different Lengths of Swords sometimes make it difficult to know the Measure, and makes it impossible to fix it by Rule, as several Masters have pretended: Some of them say that the Measure is just, when the Points cross each other a Foot; others, with as little Reason, wou'd have the Middle of your Blade touch the Point of the Adversary's; but what gives a true Knowledge of the Measure is frequent Exercise, accompanied with a good Judgment, pushing often *Quart* and *Tierce* with different Foils, and being pushed at by different Persons.

The Extention is taken from the Left-foot, which is the Centre, to the Button of the Foil.

I did design, in this Place, to treat of Time, and of a regular Way of pushing in Lessons, from the Beginning to the End of one Year, according to the Disposition of Scholars; but after I had finished it, I thought that my Fellow-Brethren would perhaps take it ill that I should prescribe Lessons to their Scholars, by which, instead of gaining their good Opinion, I might incur the Accusation of being more busy than knowing.

CHAP. XXIX.

Of the Necessity of some Qualities in a Master.

In order to teach well, it's necessary to have a perfect Idea of the Means which conduce from the Beginning to the End of the Matter proposed, I mean to it's Perfection, or to what comes nearest it, if our Age has not as yet arrived to it.

In Fencing, as well as in other Exercises, there should be Judgment and Knowledge how to act and how to Teach: The first is the Effect of a long and good Theory; the second, of a good Theory, long Practice, and a good Disposition; and the third, besides the Theory and Practice, is the Effect of a good Genius, or of a particular Talent.

Qualities which shou'd be always united; so that the Genius may be capable of teaching properly to different Persons, the Application of the Rules which are acquired by Experience.

It is as necessary in this Art that a Master's Motions shou'd be regular, and that he shou'd hold the Foil properly in his Hand, as it is for a Writing Master to draw the Example well that he would have copied; so that the Scholar of the one, or of the other, may learn a better Motion, or a finer Character. It is also proper that when a Scholar commits a Fault, the Master shou'd shame him by imitating it, the seeing the Fault making a greater Impression than the hearing of it.

A Master in his Lesson shou'd give a Time to the Scholar to make him push, in order to teach him to take the Enemy's Time. He shou'd likewise sometimes beat back his Body, and parry him from time to time, that he may accustom him to be firm on his Legs, to oppose his Sword well, and to recover well: It is good sometimes to let him make several Thrusts following, and then remaining firm all of a sudden, to shew him, that he shou'd always be ready to thrust when an Opportunity offers, and to retain himself when it does not offer.

In order to make him take the Time well, and to form his Parade and Rispost properly, the Time that the Master gives must have a Regard to Rule, and sometimes to the Disorder of an unskilful Enemy, that he may be equally fortifyed for both; and to form his Parade and Rispost the Master must push in the Manner the most like to an Assault.

Though most Masters give Lessons with shorter and stiffer Foils than are used in assaulting or playing loose, I esteem it better always to use the same Foils that they may not be deceived in an Assault.

A Master's Play shou'd be neat, subtle agreeable, and useful, as fit for Combat as for the School.

The Art of Fencing being to make the most of a good or bad Disposition, when 'tis good 'tis capable of being made perfectly dexterous, and when bad, the Defect of Nature is to be repaired by Art.

By saying that 'tis no hard Matter to perfect such Men as are naturally of a very good Disposition, is meant the bringing them to a certain Point which they could almost arrive to of themselves, by Practice and Speculation; but it is well known that it is the Business of a good Master to make his Scholar perfectly dexterous, and tho' he may have a good Disposition and long Exercise, if he is not well instructed, he cannot become dexterous, even tho' he shou'd execute with Agility, being incapable of acquiring a Good without knowing and practising it.

A good Disposition is seldom to be met with, for there is generally a Mixture of bad Parts with the good. Some have a supple, light and vigorous Body, and with these Qualities a heavy or ill adjusted Hand; and others that have as good a Disposition as is desirable, have a narrow Genius, fearing to undertake any thing, or are hot and inconsiderate, which shews that it is only be a perfect Accord of the Parts and Understanding that a Man can be perfectly dexterous.

In short an able Master does not only shew the Fault, and whence it proceeds, but also the Danger to which it exposes, and the Means to leave it. A Master whose Play is regular, or who has the best Foundation, may properly be said to be a good Master.

CHAP. XXX.

Rules for pushing and parrying at the Wall, and for making an Assault.

Though 'tis absolutely necessary to begin by way of Lesson, and to continue in it a long Time, in order that Practice growing to a Habit, may give Liberty to the Parts to form themselves: nevertheless however well you may take your Lessons, some other Means are necessary to make an Assault well, than those which the Master gives at his *Plastron*: This Rule must be supported by pushing and parrying at the Wall, and in the Manner I am going to lay down.

When you have laboured a certain Time at Lessons, you must push at a Cushion which is fixed against the Wall for that Purpose, observing the Guard, and the Measure or Extention of the Thrust; and that the Hand display itself in *Quart*, not only according to the Rule, but first, adjusting and supporting the Thrust, and that all the Parts be placed in the most advantageous Situation for the Thrust and Recovery, which shou'd be very regularly observed.

After having lunged for some Days on the Cushion, to fix the Wrist and Body a little, you must push at a Scholar, who Being placed at the Wall will parry your Thrusts; you shou'd be in Measure, and to see if it be just, you must lunge in *Quart*, placing the Button softly on the Body, at the same time taking off your Hat, having taken the Measure you must recover in Guard, and place yourself on the Outside of his Sword in order to disengage and push *Quart*, being more careful of pushing justly than hitting; he that parrys shou'd from time to time drop his Foil, which will shew whether he that pushes follows the Blade or the Line of the Body; having remain'd some Time upon the Lunge to form the Support of the Wrist and the Posture of the Body you recover to Guard. When you lunge pretty well in *Quart*, you may disengage and push *Tierce*, and when the Thrust is pushed and parryed, you may recover and push *Seconde* under.

When you have pushed for some Time in this Manner, you may practise to parry, putting yourself for that Purpose to the Wall, which furnishes a better Parade than at large, where you are used to draw back the Body which weakens it, whereas here you cannot, which makes the Parade stronger, having no Dependence but on the Foil; you shou'd chuse a Scholar that pushes the most regularly, it being difficult without that, that a Beginner shou'd learn to parry justly.

Most young Beginners endeavour to hit at any Rate, instead of practising what would be beneficial to them, but instead of deceiving others they deceive themselves, by practising less how to form themselves and push according to Rule, than how to spoil their Bodies, and destroy the Solidity of the Principles: Some use themselves to push with the Wrist only, without the Foot, which is dangerous, by reason of the too great Measure; others with as little Reason, and as much Danger, place themselves without binding the Blade, and thrust under the Wrist; in the one the Situation of the Guard is good for nothing, and in the other there is no Defence if the Adversary thrusts at that time: Others deceive by making a Time or Motion when they are placed, but the pushing at the Wall requires only the Justness and Swiftness of the Thrust; others put themselves very near baulking the Measure, which may be done four Ways, tho' the Left-foot may be in it's proper Place, and kept firm in the Thrust; the first is done by marking or bringing forward the Point of the Left-foot, keeping it a little in, then advancing the Heel, which gives more Measure; secondly, by keeping back the Body on a Lunge, you deceive the Measure and hit by abandoning it forward, which gives it a greater Extention, thirdly, by raising or carrying the Wrist too high, or too much to one Side, which shortning the Thrust, makes it believed that you are out of Reach, but according to the Rule and Line you are too much in Reach; fourthly, some take Measure by holding the Thumb on the Body of the Guard, and when they have a mind to hit they hold it on the Middle of the Handle, with the Pommel in the Hand, which also gives a greater Length.

When you have for some time used yourself to push and parry at the Wall, according to the Rules that I have laid down, you must, (tho' 'tis not the Rule of Schools, especially when you push with

Strangers,) you must I say, when you push with a Scholar of your own Master, push and parry a Thrust alternately, disengaging, and then do the same Feinting, and sometime after you shou'd make the other Thrusts, telling one another your design, which makes you execute and parry them by Rule, especially if you reflect on the Motions and Postures of the Lunges and Parades. Being a little formed to this method, you may, being warned of the Thrust, parry it, telling the Adversary where you intend your Riposte, which puts him in a condition to avoid it, and gives him room to redouble after his Parade, either strait or by a Feint, at which you are not surprised, expecting by being forewarned the Thrust he is to make, which puts you easily on your Defence and Offence: by this manner of Exercise, you may not only improve faster, but with more art, the Eye and Parts being insensibly disposed to follow the Rule, whereas without this Method, the difference that there is between a lesson of assaulting a Man who forewarns you, helps you, and lets you hit him, and another who endeavours to defend himself and hit you, is, that except the Practice of Lessons be very well taught by long exercise, you fall into a Disorder which is often owing to the want of Art more than to any Defect in Nature. The taking a Lesson well, and the Manner of Pushing and Parrying which I have just described, may be attained to by Practice only, but some other things are necessary to make an Assault well; for besides the Turn of the Body, the Lightness, Suppleness and Vigour which compose the exteriour Part, you must be stout and prudent, qualities so essential, that without them you cannot act with a good Grace, nor to the purpose. If you are apprehensive, besides, that you don't push home, or justly, fear making you keep back your Thrust, or follow the Blade, the least Motion of the Enemy disorders you, and puts you out of a Condition to hit him, and to avoid his Thrusts. Without Prudence, you cannot take the advantage of the situation, motions designs of the enemy, which changing very often, according to his Capacity and to the Measure, demonstrates that an ill concerted Enterprise exposes more to Danger than it procures Advantage: in order to turn this Quality to an advantage, you are to observe the Enemy's *fort* and *feeble*, whether he attack or defend; if he attack it will be either by plain Thrusts strait, or disengaged, or by Feints or Engagements, which may be opposed by Time, or Ripostes: if he keeps on his Defence, it is either to take the Time or to Riposte. In case of the first; you shou'd, by half Thrusts, oblige him to push in order to take a Counter to his Time, and if he sticks to his Parade you must serve in what Manner, in order to disorder him by Feints, and push where he gives Light.

It would fill a whole Volume to describe the Thrusts that may be made, according to the Difference of Persons, as well to surprise as to avoid being surprised; besides the many Repetitions wou'd be extremely puzzling, for which Reason, I have, instead of them, laid down the following Advices, which contain chiefly, what I cou'd not otherwise have communicated without a long Treatise.

- Don't put yourself in Guard within the Reach of the Enemy.

- Make no wry Faces, or Motions that are disagreeable to the

  Sight.

- Be not affected, negligent, nor stiff.

- Don't flatter yourself in your Lessons, and still less in Assaults.

- Be not angry at receiving a Thrust, but take care to avoid it.

- Be not vain at the Thrusts you give, nor shew Contempt when you receive them.

- Do not endeavour to give many Thrusts, running the Risque of receiving one.

- Don't think yourself expert, but that you may become so.

- When you present the Foils, give the Choice without pressing.

- If you are much inferiour, make no long Assaults.

The Art of Fencing

- Do nothing that's useless, every Action shou'd tend to your Advantage.

- Lessons and Assaults are only valuable when the Application and Genius make them so.

- Too good an Opinion spoils many People, and too bad a one still more.

- A natural Disposition and Practice are necessary in Lessons, but in Assaults there must be a Genius besides.

- The Goodness of Lessons and of Assaults does not consist so much in the Length as in the Manner of them.

- When you have to do with one that's bold and forward, it is necessary to seem apprehensive in order to get a favourable Opportunity.

- If you act against one that's fearful, attack him briskly to put him in Disorder.

- Before you applaud a Thrust given, examine if Chance had no Hand in it.

- Thrusts of Experience, and those of Chance are different, the first come often, the others seldom or never happen, you may depend on one, but not on the other.

- In Battle let Valour and Prudence go together, the Lyon's Courage with the Fox's Craft.

- To be in Possession of what you know, you must be in Possession of yourself.

- Undertake nothing but what your Strength and the Capacity of the Enemy will admit of in the Execution.

- The Beauty of an Assault appears in the Execution of the Design.

- Make no Thrust without considering the Advantage and the Danger of it.

- If the Eye and Wrist precede the Body, the Execution will be good.

- Be always cautious, Time lost cannot be regained.

- If you can hit without a Feint, make none, two Motions are more dangerous than one.

- To know what you risque, you must know what you are worth.

- If you would do well, acquire the agreeable and useful.

- Twenty good Qualities will not make you perfect, and one bad one will hinder your being so.

- Judge of a Thrust, rather by Reason than by it's Success; the one may fail, but the other cannot.

- To parry well is much, but it is nothing when you can do more.

- Let your Guard, and your Play be always directly opposite to the Enemy.

- Practice is either a Good or an Evil; all consists in the Choice of it.

- When you think yourself skilful and dexterous, 'tis then you are not so.

- 'Tis not enough that your Parts agree, they must also answer the Enemy's Motions.

- The knowing a Good without practising it, turns to an Evil.

- Two skilful Men acting together, fight more with their Heads than with their Hands.

- If you are superiour to your Enemy, press him close, and if you are inferiour, break Measure to keep him moving.

- Endeavour both to discover the Enemy's Design, and to conceal your own.

- When the Eye and the Hand agree in the same instant, you are perfectly right.

- Draw not your Sword, but to serve the King, preserve your Honour, or defend your Life.

CHAP. XXXI.

Against several erroneous Opinions.

Though there are People of a bad Taste in every Art or Science, there are more in that of Fencing than in others, as well by Reason of the little Understanding of some Teachers, as of the little Practice of some Learners, who are not acting upon a good Foundation, or long enough, to have a good idea of it, argue so weakly on this Exercise, that I thought it as much my Business to observe their Errors, as it is my Duty to instruct those that I have the Honour to teach in the Theory of it: By this Means, I may furnish the One with juster Sentiments, and the Others with the Means of preserving their Honour and Lives.

I begin with those, who defer letting their Children learn 'till they have attained a certain Age, Growth and Strength. If these three Qualities would enable them to put this Art in Execution immediately, I acknowledge that they ought not to begin 'till they possessed them; but it is by long Experience and Practice only, that they can become perfect; so that except they begin young, the Employments for which they are designed, may not give them Time to arrive to it; besides, by beginning in a tender Age, the Body is more easily brought to a good Air, and an easy Disengagement; being more at Liberty, and less used to Faults, which it would naturally fall into for want of being cultivated.

Others say that it is needless to learn when the Disposition is wanting, which is an Error; for a Body that is well disposed by Nature, can better dispense with the Want of Improvement, than those that she has taken less care of; these requiring a constant Labour, to acquire what the others have almost of themselves; and tho' they cannot arrive to a perfect Agility, yet their Bodies will be better disposed to act, and their Lives not so much in Danger.

Some assure you that the knowing how to Fence, makes a Man quarrelsome, and thereby exposes him to dangerous Consequences, without considering it is a natural Brutality, Honour, or Danger, which obliges him to attack another, or defend himself, which he would do without having learned, with this Difference; that though he have the same Brutality or Courage, the Issue of the Battle is not the same; and if he have Occasion to defend himself, would it not be better for him to be able to do it, than to leave his Life to an uncertain and dangerous Hazard.

Others say that it is enough to learn one Exercise at a time; that a Plurality of different Lessons fatigues the Mind and the Body: But as one Science disposes the Mind for the others, they having a Sort of a Correspondence one with another, so Exercises favour one another as well in regard to the Posture of the Body, as to the Freedom of Motion; besides, that learning them one after another, as each Particular would take up as much Time as all in general, this Length of Time would be too great for any one almost to succed in them.

Many People say that with Sword in Hand the Rules of the School are not observed, and that 'tis sufficient to have a good Heart: It is certain that People who are subject to this Error, are not capable of following the Rules which are to be acquired only by putting a good Theory in Practice; which by frequent Use, disposes the Eye and the Part of Executing so well, that it is almost impossible to act otherwise: And as to the Practice of Schools and of the Sword, 'tis the same; for no one ought to do any thing with the Foil, but what he knows by Experience to be without Risque, according to his Rules. In some Cases, it is true, what is esteemed good in one, is not in the other. For Example: Thrusts with the Foil are good only on the Body, and with the Sword they are good every where; and that in an Assault with the Foil, the joining is reckoned as nothing, whereas in Battle 'tis the Seal of the Victory; but except in that, it should be alike in every Thing.

Others say that if they had to do with experienced Men, they would not give them Time to put themselves in Guard; as if a Man who is expert were not always on his Guard, being more knowing, and better disposed, not only to place himself at once, by the Habit that all his Parts have contrasted, but also to surprise, and to avoid being surprised, by the Knowledge he has of Time and Measure: On the contrary, an unskilful Person being ignorant of both, is easily catch'd; besides, that his Parts being unaccustomed to place themselves regularly, or at once, must always be in a continual Motion, vainly seeking their Place, by which they give the Time, and would lose it if it were given to them.

Some, in Opposition to these, say that if they know how to keep themselves in Guard 'tis sufficient. They are in the right if the Guard be perfect, which is not to be acquired but by a Practice as long as is necessary to make them perfectly dexterous, which is not their Meaning; they thinking that it is only the placing of the Parts, which is useless, without Freedom and Vigour to manage them. These are Qualities which when accompanied with a certain regular Air, and a good Grace, shew, as soon as a Man takes a Sword or Foil in his Hand, to what Pitch of Dexterity he is arrived.

Some Men will tell you that they know enough to serve their Turn: Those who use this Expression, as well as those I have spoken of before, sufficiently shew that they have learnt but little or nothing. In Effect it is no hard Matter to judge of the different Degrees of Ability; so that when a Man finds himself inferiour, he cannot properly say that he knows enough to serve his Turn; and a Man who is superiour, knows very well that he is not perfect, and that if his good Disposition together with his long Practice, has brought him very forward in the Art, others may know as much as he, and that therefore he is not so perfect as an unskilful Person may imagine.

I have heard several People say that they did not care to be dexterous, nor to know the five Rules, provided they knew how to defend themselves, and to push and parry well; and really they are in the right, supposing they could do that without practising what the most able Men have invented upon this Occasion.

There are People that say, that with Sword in Hand, against an able Man, there is nothing to be done but push vigorously, to disorder him: I am apt to believe that this may succeed against a Man who is not well form'd, or has not the Courage and Resolution that is necessary; but if he has enough to keep up his Spirit, this Attack will be advantageous to him; because it cannot be done without giving him an Opportunity of getting the better; and besides, I have Reason to believe that the greatest Part of those who talk in this Manner, would hardly attempt an able Man.

It may be said that People have then fought in this Manner with Success; but as there is Difference in Persons, what succeeded with them against unskilful People or Cowards, would have been dangerous against other Men.

I have met with People who were weak enough to believe that Knowledge in Fencing takes away the Heart, saying, that seeing the Counters to every Thrust they form, by Means of that Knowledge, an Idea of evident Danger, which dissipating the Courage, and causing an Apprehension, hinders them from their Enterprise; when an unskilful Person blindly undertakes every thing. It is true that there is great Blindness in this Way of pushing, as they say, and still more in their Understanding, to think that an able Man dares not undertake or venture when the Appearance of Success leads him to it; and that an ignorant Man shall venture when his Loss is almost certain. Is it reasonable to suppose, that a Man of natural Courage shou'd lose it, because he is assured that he is more expert than his Enemy, over whom, or perhaps his Equals, he always had the Better in Assaults, by the Help of his Knowledge and Dexterity? This, far from intimidating him, seems to assure him of Success, which is due to his habitual Practice. On the contrary, an awkard Man having seen, by his Disadvantage in School Assaults, that he has no Room to hope in Combat, the dexterous Man possessing the Qualities which procure Success, and one who had never handled a Foil, will be as much puzzled, as if he had experience'd the Disadvantage of it.

Others, with as little Reason, leave all to Chance, but the very Name is sufficient to shew that it is not to be relye'd on.

Some again say to what Purpose shall we learn to Fence, the KING had forbid Duels: It is true that this great Prince, as august for his Piety as for his Victories, was willing thereby to preserve the Blood of his bravest Subjects, who expose'd it every Day to be shed through a false Notion of Honour.

But tho' he forbid Duels, he was so far from hindering the Practice of the Sword, that he has established several Academies for the perfect

Use of it, not only for Defence, but also to qualify his Subjects to put the Justice of his Measures in Execution: And it must at last be agreed to, that a Man who wears a Sword, without knowing how to use it, runs as great a Hazard, and is full as ridiculous, as a Man who carries Books about him without knowing how to read.

Many Men are of Opinion that a Man may naturally know enough to attack or defend himself, without the Assistance of Art: Man, tho' the only reasonable Creature, finds himself deprived of what irrational Creatures naturally possess; and he requires for his Improvement the Assistance and Practice of others; the grand Art of War, and that of using the Sword, which has been practised thro' so many Ages, still find new Inventions; and it may be said, that as there is no Place, in whatever Situation by Nature, but requires Art to secure it's Defence; so likewise, whatever Disposition a Man possesses, he cannot be perfect without the Assistance of Rules and Practice.

Some Men acknowledge that Skill is necessary in single Combat, but that in a Crowd or Battle it is altogether useless: I own that on these Occasions, it is less useful than in single Battle, by reason of the different Accidents, as of Cannon, Musquets, and of other Arms; besides, a Man may be attacked by several at once: But if a Man cannot avoid being hit with a Ball, and sometimes with a Sword, he may, nevertheless, by the Disposition and Agility of the Parts, more easily defend and return a Thrust: Besides, being more able to hit with the Edge or Point, he may put more Enemies to flight, or keep them at a greater Distance. If the French Troops have always been victorious, Sword in Hand, a Part of the Glory is owing to the Skill of several Officers; and I'll venture to say, that if they had all been as expert as they should have been, you might see, as well on Foot as on Horseback, in Battle as on a Breach, Actions that would be not only uncommon but prodigious. It may perhaps be said, that our Enemies have some expert Officers among them; besides, that their Number is commonly less than in *France*, there is as great a Difference between their Dexterity and that of the *French*, as between their Masters and our's, from whom very few would have learned if the War had no suspended our Academies.[5]

I think it proper to finish this Chapter by confuting an Error as common, and more ridiculous, than the others; which is, of an infallible Thrust, which a great many People think that Masters reserve for dangerous Occasions, or to sell it at a dear Rate. This wonderful Thing, is called the secret Thrust. I don't know whether this Error proceeded from those who have not learned, or from the Chimera of some self-conceited Masters, who have sold to ignorant Scholars, some Thrusts as infallible, of their own Contrivance, as ridiculous and dangerous as the Simplicity of the Scholar and the Knavery of the Master are great.

To discover the Error of this Opinion you must observe two Things: First, that in Fencing there are no more than five Thrusts or Places, which I have described in Page 27, shewing the Parade of each of them; and secondly, that there is no Motion without it's Opposite; so that as you cannot push without a Motion, there is no Thrust without it's Counter, and even several; for besides the different Positions of the Body, there is not only the Time to take, but also several Parades to favour the Risposts, which plainly shews, that doing one of these Things properly, this imaginary infallible Thrust, far from succeeding will expose him that would make it.

All the Secrets in the Thrusts that are given by an able Man, far from being an Effect of the Thrust, is only an Effect of the Occasion, and the Swiftness; or rather of the judgment and Practice: By Means of these Qualities all Thrusts are secret ones, or they wou'd be worth nothing.

All the Thrusts in Fencing are equally good, when they are made according to Rule, with Swiftness, and on the Occasions proper to them; wherefore they ought not to be neglected whilst the Time of learning them offers; not but you may stick closer to some Thrusts than to others, either because you may be better disposed for them, or because you are more used to them.

I thought that after I had exposed the Errors of several Persons, I might tell them, that it is contrary to the Rules of good Breeding, to talk of Things they do not understand; that oftentimes People, by their first Appearance, have been thought to possess the Qualities of knowing Men, but have afterwards forfeited the good Opinion which they had at first imposed on others.

FINIS.

Thrusts of Emulation for Prizes, Wagers &c.

All Thrusts from the Neckband to the Wastband are counted good.

Coup Fourrés or interchanged Thrusts are not counted on either side, except one of the Competitors has Recourse to it in order to make the Thrusts equal, then the Thrust of the other is good, and not his.

If one hits the Body and the other the Face or below the Wast at the same Time; the Thrust on the Body is counted, but not the other.

If a Man parrys with his Hand, and afterwards hit, his Thrust is not good, because by parrying with the Hand, his Antagonist's Foil is less at Liberty than if he had parryed with the Blade, and might be a Reason why he could not parry and risposte.

If a Man takes the Time, opposing with the Left-hand, and hits without receiving, his Thrust is not good, because if he had not Opposed with the Hand, both would have hit, the Opposition of the Hand serving only to avoid, but no way contributing to the Success of the Thrust.

If in parrying, binding, or lashing the Foil, it Falls, and that the Thrust is made without Interval, it is Good.

Thrusts made with the Sword in both hands, or shifting from one Hand to the other are not good.

A Master is not to give judgment for his own Scholar.

FOOTNOTES:

[1]

The Iron at the End of the Blade that runs into the Handle.

[2]

I am not of Opinion that the Body should be drawn back, except it be impossible to avoid the Thrust without doing it; all Parades being best when the body is not disorder'd.

[3]

See the 8th. Plate.

[4]

See the 12th Plate.

[5]

As in this Paragraph, Monsieur L'Abbat rather introduces an Encomium on his Country-men, than any thing essential to the Art of Fencing. I leave the Reader to his own Opinion thereon.

Lightning Source UK Ltd.
Milton Keynes UK
UKOW02f1811020815

256249UK00001B/46/P